The Crucificado

Also by Edgar White

UNDERGROUND: Four Plays
SATI: The Rastafarian (Children's Book)

The Crucificado

Two Plays

by Edgar White

William Morrow & Company, Inc.
New York 1973

ISBN 0-688-00044-4
ISBN 0-688-05044-1 (pbk)

*To Adrienne Kennedy and
Sam Rivers, musician*

Contents

The Life and Times
of J. Walter Smintheus

To Owen Dodson, William Demby and Earle Hyman

Characters

J. WALTER SMINTHEUS, *a historian-sociologist (black)*
JOYCE, *Smintheus's wife (black)*
ROBERT, *Smintheus's friend (black)*
MARGIE, *Smintheus's mistress (black)*
BOB, *Margie's friend (white)*
EDWARD, *Smintheus's brother-in-law (white)*
DR. COMMA, *president of a Southern college (black)*
KARL *and* LENA, *friends of Smintheus and Joyce (black)*
DINERS, WAITER, *and* MANAGER, *at restaurant (white)*
MALE SANITARIUM PATIENT
TWO DWARFS

THE LIFE AND TIMES OF J. WALTER SMINTHEUS *was produced at the New York Shakespeare Public Theater in April, 1971. Walter Jones was the director. The play was showcased at ANTA in February, 1971, with Earle Hyman ,playing the title role.*

Cast members and their roles are as follows:

J. WALTER SMINTHEUS	DENNIS TATE
JOYCE	NORMA DARDEN
ROBERT	WALTER JONES
MARGIE	ROBIN BRAXTON
DR. COMMA	JOHN MOORE

Act 1

Scene 1

[The first three bars of Thelonious Monk's "Jackie-ing" are heard. The location: a sanitarium. The patient, J. Walter Smintheus, is seated in a rocking chair. He is in a catatonic state and rocks mechanically. We know his thoughts by means of a tape recorder. Smintheus is of an indeterminate age: the eyes betray a certain youth, yet a plethora of wrinkles and the tension of his face make it impossible to determine his exact age.]

SMINTHEUS: How still everything is. I've been here for some time now. Mozart comes through the walls. Perhaps someone plays him in a nearby room. But I only hear that when it's growing dark. They must only play him at evening.

How could I have gotten here? Perhaps Joyce brought me, although she isn't strong enough to have lifted me. It must have been some men. I don't remember any men though. There was that woman in a white dress that comes in to feed me. She places something around my neck. I think it's a bib. She's always talking. I don't know what she says. I can tell when she's coming because she has the heavy squeaky shoes. There's another one that's thinner. She isn't skinny really but she is a lot thinner than the fat one. She moves my rocking chair and sweeps. Sometimes she changes the flowers. I wonder if someone sends me flowers. Who would send me flowers? It couldn't be Robert because Robert is dead. The dead don't send flowers. Do they? No, dead people don't send flowers. It rains sometimes and then the raindrops make small fingers running down.

It seems that there is a great deal I must have forgotten. (*Pause.*) I must have known a lot of things at some point. There are these words. These big words that keep coming back. "Negritude." (*Pause.*) "Putrefaction." They must have come from somewhere. I must have been very bright once. I must have been intelligent. Why? Because I have these words. (*Pause.*) Where could I have gotten them from? Do I want to go to the toilet? I don't think so. But I didn't think so the other time either, but then this wet warm stuff came running down my legs and the fat woman scolded me. She scolded me and pointed to the puddle. Then that doctor with the beard came and breathed on me.

I wonder what I did before? I must have done something before. They wouldn't take care of me if I didn't do something important at some time. "Societal," that's another one that keeps coming into my head. If I lean back just a little (*he leans back in the rocking chair*), then there's no pain in my back. (*Pause.*) There, that's nice. Cross the legs like this. (*He crosses his legs.*) Ah, yes, that's it. That's not so bad now. Everything smells like alcohol. I wonder. I wonder who I am. (*Pause.*) It couldn't be very important or they would have told me. (*Pause.*) Perhaps they have told me and I've forgotten. I wonder when they'll throw me out of here. I must be careful that they don't catch me making any more puddles. I could say that a dog did it. Perhaps they are looking at me now. (*Pause.*) If they tell me who I am again, I'll make a special point of remembering. (*Pause.*) Maybe it's a three-syllable name. That would be hard to remember. But maybe it's only two. (*Pause.*) I'll remember the next time. I think.

[*Darkness.*]

Scene 2

[*Smintheus's room at Cornell University. Smintheus is seated upon his bed and does several desultory exercises. First he flexes his arms, then fingers, finally legs. Utters an Oblomovian sigh, and proceeds to pull on his clothes. A knock is heard at the door.*]

SMINTHEUS: Come in.

[*It is Edward, a severe, Protestant-looking Yalie.*]

Oh, Edward.

EDWARD: Hello, Smintheus.

SMINTHEUS: Care for some *café au lait*, Edward? I take a bit of honey in mine. Quite good, really.

EDWARD: All right. I'll try it. Look, it's about your sister.

SMINTHEUS: Oh.

EDWARD: Yes. (*He sits down on a chair or the bed;*

Smintheus sits in a rocker.) As you know, we've been seeing each other for about a year now.

SMINTHEUS: Is it that long? (*Pause.*) Yes, I guess it must be a year already.

EDWARD: We've gotten quite fond of each other. She's stayed with me, or rather, with us at my parents' home several times.

SMINTHEUS: Yes.

EDWARD: Yes, and eh, well, Mom and Dad have been most understanding about everything.

SMINTHEUS: Understanding?

EDWARD: Yes, I mean about me seeing her. And, well, I've been thinking about marriage.

SMINTHEUS: Marriage?

EDWARD: Yes, marriage.

SMINTHEUS: Marriage? (*Pause.*) Marriage.

EDWARD: Why do you keep saying it over and over?

SMINTHEUS: Oh, I was just thinking how the word sounds so much like "mirage."

EDWARD: Well, I wanted your advice, Smintheus.

SMINTHEUS: My advice?

EDWARD: Yes, I think we have been very friendly in the past, and I've a great deal of respect for your (*pause*) mind.

[8]

SMINTHEUS: My mind?

EDWARD: Yes. Your mind.

SMINTHEUS: Have you spoken with Myrna about marriage?

EDWARD: Well, no, not yet.

SMINTHEUS: So you've only spoken to your parents and me about marriage?

EDWARD: Well, I'm sure she'll be willing.

SMINTHEUS: Oh.

EDWARD: What do you think?

SMINTHEUS: I think if you both want to get married it's your affair, and you both should deal with it.

EDWARD: (*relieved*) Oh my, good; yes, it's our affair. But do you approve?

SMINTHEUS: You act as if I had some say in the matter.

EDWARD: Well, you do.

SMINTHEUS: All right, then, I approve.

EDWARD: Wonderful, wonderful. Listen: next week is the Easter vacation recess. Why don't you come down to Jamaica? My parents have a house there. It will be lots of fun. Do you play tennis?

SMINTHEUS: Not very well.

EDWARD: Golf?

SMINTHEUS: Well, I'm not very good at sports.

EDWARD: Oh, I thought you'd be so . . . oh well, why don't you come anyway?

SMINTHEUS: Well, I'll be rather busy. I have . . .

[A knock is heard at the door: a Black student, rather old-looking for a student, breaks into the room excitedly.]

ROBERT: Smintheus. Oh, excuse me.

EDWARD: It's all right. I have to get back to Yale by this afternoon. I'll be leaving. Do try to come down, Smintheus.

SMINTHEUS: All right, Edward; I'll try.

[Edward exits.]

ROBERT: Hey, man, can I borrow some money? It's important. I can't explain now.

SMINTHEUS: All right, Robert. Would you care for some coffee?

ROBERT: Your usual *café au lait*, eh?

SMINTHEUS: Yeah. How much do you need?

ROBERT: About three hundred.

SMINTHEUS: Three hundred? I'm afraid all I have is about two hundred. Dad's been rather parsimonious of late.

ROBERT: All right. I'll take it.

SMINTHEUS: (*offering Robert a cup of coffee*) A little honey, Robert?

ROBERT: No. I don't have time for coffee. Why do you always call me Robert? Everyone else calls me Bob.

SMINTHEUS: I don't know, I find Bob a little familiar, don't you?

ROBERT: I suppose. I don't know.

SMINTHEUS: (*sitting back in the rocking chair*) You know, Robert, I genuinely do not understand Caucasians.

ROBERT: You mean white people?

SMINTHEUS: Well, yes, I mean white people.

ROBERT: There's nothing to understand. Just remember, they have no use for you. And you'll be on the right track. I don't know why the hell you should worry about understanding them, when they don't even consider understanding you.

SMINTHEUS: Well, take that fellow Edward who just left. He came to speak to me about marrying my sister. Wanted my advice; he hasn't even considered the fact that she might not want to marry him.

ROBERT: Of course he hasn't considered it. If you owned the world you wouldn't consider it either.

SMINTHEUS: Well, I suppose you're right.

ROBERT: Anyway, I'm sure she'll marry him and castrate him just the way he wants.

SMINTHEUS: You've been taking too many psychology courses, Robert.

ROBERT: Listen, man, when a white man marries a black bourgeoise, he wants to be castrated.

SMINTHEUS: That's not a very nice way to speak about my sister.

ROBERT: Listen, she'll have him leaving his balls at the door after the first six weeks.

SMINTHEUS: I should have thought it might take a bit longer.

ROBERT: Do you believe in intermarriage?

SMINTHEUS: I don't believe in anything. How could I believe in intermarriage?

ROBERT: Oh, that's right. You believe everything hopeless, I forgot. (*He begins to shiver.*)

SMINTHEUS: Are you all right, Robert? You look feverish.

ROBERT: I'm all right. Listen, I need that money.

SMINTHEUS: All right. (*He takes his wallet out of his jacket pocket.*) Here you are; I'm sorry I don't have more. Are you coming to the game this afternoon?

ROBERT: No. No. I'm going back to the city for a few days. I'll see you. Thanks again.

SMINTHEUS: All right, Robert, goodbye.

[Darkness.]

Scene 3

SMINTHEUS: How shall I begin? "Dear Robert." No. "My dear friend. I am sorry to hear that you have been arrested." (*He ponders.*) Perhaps, "I know it must be difficult for you to endure prison." Too serious. (*He throws down the pen.*) Goddammit, Robert, how could you be so stupid? You're not like the others. (*He slowly picks up the pen and tries again.*) "How far away your world is. It's too desperate for me." (*Long pause.*) No. Perhaps if I make mention of the weather. Something offhand. "It rained a great deal here . . . last week." No, I'll start with something about graduation exercises. He'll like that.

[Darkness.]

Scene 4

[Two spotlights divide the stage, one on Smintheus at his desk writing, the second on Robert in prison. There is an optical illusion of bars in the background. Smintheus reads his letters aloud, then Robert does the same. Robert is dressed in a gray workshirt.]

SMINTHEUS: "Dear Robert, I write to you in this rather unfortunate circumstance. Do forgive me for being so bold as to write you at your present domicile, but I have awaited some missive from you for over five months, hearing nothing. Thus I have taken the liberty of finding out your habitation.

"I attended graduation exercises last week. All went well. President Perkins made an admirable speech about the destiny of the scholar. I was moved as I'm sure you would have been. Later, Susan Barlow had a party which I attended. She played Schumann's 'Carnaval' rather well. She's an excellent pianist although she seemed uncertain in the second movement. My parents came up from Atlanta, together with my sister Myrna and her husband Edward. (I neglected to ask him if he had lost his balls yet. He might have thought it impertinent.)

"I have moved to New York (a distressingly unclean city) and start Columbia grad school in September. My father wants me to go into business with him. However, I find the occupation of mortician a bit lacking in amusement. I'll continue in sociology or something.

"I find it rather astounding that you entered Columbia while beset with the problems of addiction. Moreover, that you managed to maintain a B+ average. It would make an excellent novel. I imagine that it is not amusing living a novel.

"I, for my part, find this life to be unkind. As Hobbes said: 'The life of man is . . . brutish and short.' Not short enough, however, I suspect. Yet we have to do something to use up our threescore and ten. So do write to me. Perhaps you'll find the exchange of epistles not unpleasant. Yours, J. Walter Smintheus.

"P.S. My new address is 412 West 116th Street, New York City."

ROBERT: "To: J. Walter Smintheus. Relationship: Friend. Dear Smintheus: I neglected to write you earlier because, well, I imagine you know why. It is good hearing from you though. I'm glad to hear all went well at good old Cornell. I miss your *café au lait*, your bright socks, and the ivy room at the Straight. All of that was unreal but anyway it was nice while it lasted.

"It occurs to me, however, that you do not seem to have the slightest idea that we are both trapped. All black people are in prison, whether they realize it or not. The first time I met you coming out of McGraw Hall, I could see in your eyes the same animal furtiveness that was in mine. That is, in the eyes of all black students at big Ivy League colleges. We know we don't belong there. We know we're freaks. We all look guilty. You came from the bourgeoisie of Atlanta. I came from the ghetto of New York, but we're all in the same boat. We're too intelligent; we don't belong. It's time that you started realizing what and who you are, and try to find something relevant to your people. (And by 'your people' I don't mean that out-to-lunch Uncle Tom father of yours.) 'See Smintheus, see Smintheus run for the white man.' Find out who you are, Smintheus. You're in New York now. Look around you. Yours in revolution, Robert."

SMINTHEUS: "I say, Robert, I thought your remarks about my father excessively familiar. Likewise your comment about 'animally furtive eyes.' I thought it a bit much. Doubtless what you saw in my eyes was the result of myopia (an illness to which several people in my family are prone). I will not argue the point further, however. I will have to agree with you as to the point of entrapment of the Negro race. We are to an inordinate degree held down. However, whether or not we are all in identical circumstances is a moot point.

"You, for example, weep for the misery of our race. I, on the other hand, weep for myself. My melancholia has to do with the fact that I find no one in this world to speak with who is as interesting as myself. I am always circumscribed by the dull and tedious who are always in power.

"I will, nonetheless, as you say, attempt to find out more about our people. Yours in insurrection, J. Walter.

"P.S. I should be interested to know something of your environment. Tell me, do you wear that striped garb that one always sees in cartoons? I'm sending a few books along which may perhaps help you to pass the time."

ROBERT: "Dear Smintheus, The life of man may be more than seventy years. Remember, certain slaves lived to be a hundred or more.

"You want to know something of my conditions here, do you? Well, I'm in a cell block with about four hundred others. I can't go into too much detail, lest the censors become nervous. There are two to a cell (where there should be one). There is some sort of priestcraft here—two guards are like priests, the warden is the Pope. I needn't speak of the food; suffice to call it atrocious. If there is any doubt in your mind as to the function of prisons in America, let me state that they are almost solely made for the purpose of suppressing black people. Blacks make up ninety percent of the prisoners here. Make what you will of that, Mr. Sociologist. Yours (and by the way, ass, it's revolution, not insurrection), Robert."

[Darkness.]

Scene 5

[Two Dwarfs cross the stage holding a sign: "Smintheus Falls in Love." Smintheus is in his apartment. He is in his rocking chair; his girlfriend Joyce sits beside him in an armchair. On the wall is a plaque reading: "Earth, Water, Fire, and Air."]

JOYCE: Smintheus.

SMINTHEUS: Yes?

JOYCE: Do you believe in love?

SMINTHEUS: No.

JOYCE: I mean, don't you think it's possible?

SMINTHEUS: I don't.

JOYCE: You don't what?

SMINTHEUS: Think.

JOYCE: We've been seeing each other for a very long time now.

SMINTHEUS: You remember Robert, don't you?

JOYCE: You mean Bob, the drug addict?

SMINTHEUS: I wish you wouldn't call him that.

[17]

JOYCE: Yes, I remember him from Cornell. I never liked him. Didn't he rob you?

SMINTHEUS: Unimportant.

JOYCE: I don't think so. Why do Negroes always have to hurt their own people?

SMINTHEUS: Because they never get a chance to hurt the white race, that's all. If they could they would.

JOYCE: How can you not believe in love?

SMINTHEUS: It's a shame he got himself in this mess; he's a very brilliant fellow.

JOYCE: Smintheus, look at me.

SMINTHEUS: What?

JOYCE: I said look at me. It's time for us to stop fooling around and either do it or stop seeing each other.

SMINTHEUS: Oh, fine. Are you finally ready to go to bed with me?

JOYCE: I mean get married. People do that, you know. It's a means of propagating the race.

SMINTHEUS: That's what's wrong with it.

JOYCE: What do you have against people?

SMINTHEUS: They bore me.

JOYCE: Smintheus, let's get married. I'll make you happy. I know I will.

SMINTHEUS: Happy? What's happy?

JOYCE: Happy. You know: enjoy your life, enjoy being with another person. Like *normal people.* You can do your work—I won't hinder you.

SMINTHEUS: What work?

JOYCE: Well, whatever it is you do with all those books up there. After all, you're going to get a Ph.D. next year. You've obviously got something. Let me take care of you.

SMINTHEUS: Well, if I agree to marriage, does that mean we're engaged starting now?

JOYCE: (*excitedly*) Oh, Smintheus, yes. We're engaged. We can get a ring.

SMINTHEUS: Can I have some now?

JOYCE: Smintheus.

SMINTHEUS: Well, I at least want to know what I'm getting into.

JOYCE: Well, you don't make it sound very romantic.

SMINTHEUS: Well, I'm sorry, I've never gotten married before. Can we go to bed now?

JOYCE: (*laughing*) All right. (*She starts to unbutton her dress. Well-shaped, Southern bourgeoise; her manner must be refined.*)

SMINTHEUS: Well, threescore and ten may not be so bad.

   [Darkness.]

Scene 6

[Smintheus is again seated at his desk. The same situation as in Scene 3: bars in background and two spotlights on Smintheus and Robert.]

SMINTHEUS: "Dear Robert, It seems as though I'm to be married. My bride is of the Philadelphia Dubois, the perfume merchants. We are to be married in June (she likes that) and will honeymoon in Paris for the summer. She is very good in bed and wants children. We disagree on *that* point but I do believe we shall reach some equitable agreement. I have no intention of bringing any child into this filthy and unkind world for the sake of a three-minute erection. She is a kind enough girl, though. She doesn't understand my sadness, but her heart is in the right place. Whatever the hell that means. My sister has given birth to a bouncing nappy-headed boy named John Philip Edward Wilson. They are apparently very gleeful about this. I am now an uncle. I've placed a bond in his name in the First National City Bank. He certainly won't need it (he's already enrolled at Yale), but in any case it was a gesture.

"I will send you many colorful postcards from Paris. Perhaps you can decorate your cell. Upon my return I will see about securing a teaching position at Spilth College in Tennessee. I'm curious to see the workings of these small Negro colleges. Joyce remembers you from Cornell. Do you remember her? She was in our English class. Of course she never spoke. You know how women treat English as a foreign language.

"Carry on. Yours, J. Walter."

ROBERT: "Dear Eunuch, I was happy, or at least entertained, to hear that you have followed the pattern. As you may or may not know there is a pattern with the black intelligentsia: There is a certain point where you marry either a white girl who wants to save *you*, or *you* her. Or—you marry a black bourgeoise, some girl who decides you're going to be important someday and comes along for the ride. She dominates you, she misunderstands you, she castrates you, and then she leaves you. Don't worry, though, they're good for keeping houses neat, filled with *art nouveau*, good for cocktail parties. They make petite children and don't start going to analysts until after the first year of marriage. There will be the trips to Europe and then eventually a total departure to a Scandinavian country, where you will almost be able to totally forget you're black. Your life will be, if nothing else, constant. Yours in prison, Robert.

"P.S. Mortician marries Perfume."

[Darkness.]

Act 2

Scene 1

[The two Dwarfs come out holding a sign reading "Smintheus Teaches."

The scene opens to reveal a huge desk with several men seated about on chairs. They are all overweight and have graying or grayed hair and mustaches. They wear the same suits and should look as alike as possible.

A knock is heard.]

DR. COMMA: Come in. Ah, come in, Smintheus. Do you know these gentlemen? They are our trustees—Dr. Warner, Dr. Philips, Mr. Hugo, and Mr. Grant.

SMINTHEUS: How do you do?

[They all stand and sit in unison.]

DR. COMMA: Smintheus.

SMINTHEUS: Yes, Dr. Comma.

DR. COMMA: Do you like it here, Smintheus?

SMINTHEUS: Like it here?

DR. COMMA: Yes, Smintheus. I mean, are you happy?

SMINTHEUS: I'm sorry, but you'll have to define your terms.

DR. COMMA: What terms, Smintheus?

SMINTHEUS: Like what you mean by happy. I don't re-member feeling that emotion for the last twenty-eight years.

DR. COMMA: You know what I mean, Smintheus. Are you satisfied here?

SMINTHEUS: Yes, I'm reasonably satisfied.

MR. GRANT: Then why the hell are you . . .

DR. COMMA: Please, Mr. Grant, I'll take care of this. Smintheus . . .

SMINTHEUS: Yes, Dr. Comma.

DR. COMMA: You're working on a study.

SMINTHEUS: Yes, sir, in five volumes.

DR. COMMA: Entitled *The Contributions of the Negro Intellectual to American Society and His Resultant Im-potence.*

SMINTHEUS: Yes, sir.

DR. COMMA: You think the Negro intellectual in America is totally impotent?

SMINTHEUS: I think he is. In fact, he doesn't exist, sir. To the white power structure.

DR. COMMA: The white power structure? Are you a Communist, Smintheus?

SMINTHEUS: Not that I remember, sir.

DR. COMMA: Not that you remember. Mm hmm. Tell me, Smintheus, I understand you're organizing students to strike.

SMINTHEUS: No, sir.

DR. COMMA: No?

SMINTHEUS: No, sir. I'm merely assisting the striking students, sir. I've agreed to represent their demands.

DR. COMMA: Oh, merely assisting.

SMINTHEUS: Yes, sir.

DR. COMMA: Smintheus, I think it might be more advantageous for you to teach at another college.

SMINTHEUS: Advantageous for whom, sir?

DR. COMMA: Advantageous for everyone, Smintheus. And stop calling me "sir."

SMINTHEUS: I'm sorry, sir, I detest familiarity.

DR. COMMA: What do you and those students hope to gain by disrupting classes? Do you like these rebels so much that you'd be willing to lose your job for them?

SMINTHEUS: Well, sir, I'll tell you. No, I do not like these students very much. They are crass, crude, and ill-learned. But the reason they are so backward is because of people like you who maintain inferior institutions and haven't changed your curriculum in a hundred years. God bless good old Booker T. Washington. And George Washington Carver. They meant well, but their day is over. Your college isn't worth even a Northern high school. Which isn't to say that the Northern high schools are good—just that your college is exceptionally bad. It's good that it is exceptionally something, but unfortunate that it has to be exceptionally bad.

DR. COMMA: I know what the problem is. I know what it is. See, you've lived away from home too long. Evidently you have forgotten what we are all about down here. Yes, I have made a personal error with you, Smintheus, and that is something quite uncommon for me.

SMINTHEUS: Error?

DR. COMMA: Yes, I can usually spot someone who is going to make trouble for me a mile off. I naturally thought it would be to the good of the college to hire someone from one of the better . . . from one of the more prestigious Ivy League schools up North. And well, you being, after all, an adequate scholar and an Omega man, I naturally assumed you would benefit us. (*Pause.*) By the way, you are an Omega man, aren't you, Smintheus?

SMINTHEUS: Yes, sir, and my wife's a Delta.

DR. COMMA: You see, Smintheus, you have no idea how much I had to go through to achieve this position. I assure you it wasn't easy. Do you know the last four presidents to precede me were octoroons? All four of them.

SMINTHEUS: My goodness.

DR. COMMA: As you can plainly see, I'm dark, Smintheus. It was considerably harder for me. I set my mind to the mark, and didn't flinch until I had attained it. You see, Smintheus, how foolhardy it would be for me to allow you to destroy everything I've labored for in the name of change.

SMINTHEUS: Yes, sir.

DR. COMMA: You see, the Southern university functions as a parent to its student body. We pride ourselves in providing a moral as well as an intellectual standard for our students. We provide a sturdy base upon which to build responsible men and women of color—the future Alain Lockes, Philip Randolphs, and Thurgood Marshalls. We accustom them to hard work, and we especially prepare them for the difficult realities of the outside world.

SMINTHEUS: By insisting that they attend chapel daily?

DR. COMMA: Yes, we make chapel mandatory for our students. We function as a parent here, Smintheus. We are concerned with making the total person, not just the educated person—they don't understand that up North. I made a personal error with you, Smintheus.

SMINTHEUS: Sorry, sir.

DR. COMMA: I think you'd best move on, Smintheus.

SMINTHEUS: Thank you, sir, it's been . . . educational.

[Darkness.]

[26]

Scene 2

[The Dwarfs cross the stage bearing a sign: "All Is Not Well with Smintheus." The scene opens with dual location, as before.]

SMINTHEUS: "Dear Robert: Have secured lodging on West 86th Street. Am doing very well with my study. Have finished the first volume, which deals with Negro contributions from the American Revolution to the beginning of Negro banks and insurance companies, post-Abolition. The second volume should cover from 1890 to 1930. My experience at Spilth College has helped me immeasurably. I've had trouble with Joyce. She doesn't understand what I'm trying to do. All has not been well with me. My father apparently died two weeks ago, on the seventh of November. It surprised me. I didn't expect that right now.

"I have to find out more about jazz. I've come to the strange realization that it's the only genuine American art form. Pity that you're in prison now. You could have been quite helpful.

"I do miss Europe, Robert, Paris especially. Reading Verlaine in the Luxembourg Gardens. I'm going to have to get some sort of job eventually, I can't stand the vapid faces of students anymore. I'll have to try something other than teaching. Robert, this . . ."

ROBERT: (*a soliloquy*) Life's sometimes not easy under colonialism. It makes people (*pause*) whisper, or drink, or take dope. It's not easy. It sometimes makes you have to go to the master's museum to see the history of your race on exhibit behind plate glass. A single man may own your entire history. You know. I mean it makes things kind of uncertain. Colonialism. It allows people to get wakened from their beds at strange hours. And sometimes they're forced into the streets naked.

Colonialism is sometimes awkward for the master; I mean how can he look into your eyes, he feels so guilty. That's why no one is allowed a face under colonialism. No faces. Hey there, you, where's your ID? Come on, show us your papers. What, you think you're free or something?

Colonialism. Women seem to get along better than men under colonialism. (*He reflects for a moment.*) No, that's not true, women wear pain better than men. Women know the most about it. They have to lie under the belly of colonialism. My woman goes out, she has to steal for me, I'm not allowed to get close enough. We're different to them. My body looks like the streets. It's worn like the streets. Hers still looks new. They can deal with that.

Colonialism makes you want to kill people, and keep on killing. And you know it's at the back of everyone's mind. And they never say it. They'd like you to just quietly go off and die some place. Send in a team of sociologists to catalog you.

The clothes that you wear. The costumes of colonialism. Just what is the well-dressed colonialist wearing these days? And how does his lady see herself today? Part of which fantasy?

And what is the costume of the happy slave today?

You can be a happy slave, or remembered as an unhappy one. Remember me as being a very, very unhappy slave.

[Darkness.]

SMINTHEUS: (*continuing*) ". . . life is a strange thing. If something untoward should happen to me, please see to my book. I would be obliged. That's all that matters now.

"I have been plagued of late by nightmares wherein certain men awaken me and force me to appear before God. My face is looking more like my father's every day. I don't know quite what it means. Yours, J. Walter."

ROBERT: "Dear Smintheus, Thank you for the books. Don't think I don't appreciate them. However, Kant's *Critique of Pure Reason* is not exactly what I need now. If you could just send a few simple magazines and perhaps a carton of cigarettes, I think that they might be a bit more useful to me. I'm glad to hear your work is going well. You shouldn't have much trouble getting it published because they won't understand it and no one will take it seriously. Keep working, Brother. Yours, Robert."

[Darkness.]

Scene 3

[Smintheus is seated at his desk. He reads and writes with his eyes only a few inches away from the paper. (He is extremely nearsighted by now.) Joyce enters. She is four years older than when they married and looks it. She calls him. He does not respond.]

JOYCE: (*drawing closer*) Smintheus. (*Louder.*) Smintheus. (*No response. She goes over to him and calls right into his ear, separating the syllables of his name.*) Smin-the-us.

SMINTHEUS: (*looking up and turning around*) Yes, dear. Did you want something?

JOYCE: Yes, your wife would like to speak with you for a minute if you'll be so kind.

SMINTHEUS: Go on, Joyce-Ann. What is it?

JOYCE: And stop calling me Joyce-Ann. You know I hate that.

SMINTHEUS: Sorry, Joyce. Go ahead. But please, do make it brief.

JOYCE: Smintheus. (*She starts pacing slowly.*) Tell me, doesn't your father's inheritance strike you as strange?

SMINTHEUS: Strange? No.

JOYCE: Well, the fact that he only left you five hundred dollars.

SMINTHEUS: Well, you know, the business was doing poorly for the last few years.

JOYCE: But he left your sister fifteen thousand and she sure doesn't need it. She's got a great big white husband whose parents are millionaires. And he left your mother twenty-five thousand plus all that property.

SMINTHEUS: How do you know how much he left my sister and my mother?

JOYCE: Your sister called and told me.

SMINTHEUS: Well, apparently everyone in the world knows more than I do.

JOYCE: Why would he only leave you five hundred?

SMINTHEUS: Well, Dad and I never saw eye to eye on several things.

JOYCE: Like when he said you were destined to be a no-good bum.

SMINTHEUS: Well, I don't know if he called me a no-good bum exactly.

JOYCE: I do. Remember when you gave him that box of Danish cigars on his birthday and he asked you what you were going to do with yourself after all that damn money he spent on your education.

SMINTHEUS: Oh yeah—I answered that I said I didn't know what I wanted to do.

JOYCE: Right—and that's when he called you a no-good bum and said you'd probably bring the family to ruin. Still, he could have made it more than five hundred dollars.

SMINTHEUS: Well, he could have made it fifty cents if he really wanted to. Joyce, I have to get back to my work now.

JOYCE: Smintheus, why don't we go to the Johnsons' party?

SMINTHEUS: Party?

JOYCE: Yes, you know, in Queens. It will give me a chance to wear that new dress that you said you liked so much.

SMINTHEUS: Where is Queens?

JOYCE: It's somewhere near New York. They've got a very nice house in St. Albans. I'm sure we could find it.

SMINTHEUS: I really can't, honey. I've got another forty pages to get done today. I'm almost finished with the third volume.

JOYCE: The third volume, damn it! That's all I ever hear: the third volume. I would like a husband for a change. (*She storms out of the room.*)

[*Smintheus pauses a moment, looks quizzical, and then returns to his papers.*]

[*Darkness.*]

Scene 4

[*Smintheus and Joyce are visiting friends in Queens. The number of people visible is optional. Lena, the hostess, is urbane and buoyant. Karl, one of the guests, has come without his wife.*]

LENA: I am so glad that you could make it, Joyce. You two have been almost invisible since you moved to New York.

KARL: (*engaged in conversation with Smintheus*) No, but you see what I mean, Smintheus, they don't have the right to judge us.

SMINTHEUS: I understand what you're saying but . . .

JOYCE: Who doesn't have the right?

KARL: The young people don't have the right to judge us because they have no idea what the circumstances were surrounding our choices and actions.

LENA: Please, you make me feel old when you speak about the young people as if they were a separate race.

KARL: No, it just makes me angry when a young nappy-headed revolutionary type, you know, who looks as if he hasn't seen a barber in three years and stinks of the grass roots, tells me that I'm not black enough. Where was he when it was not fashionable to be black and poor? They have no idea what we went through. I got an ulcer being black and trying to deal with the realities of the white world. You know how hard it was for us in the thirties and forties. And it wasn't so easy to be yourself and survive. It was damn lonely out there. You know how the socialists were using us. Nobody cared for or about the Negro.

LENA: Especially not the Negro.

KARL: Thank you. Negroes surely weren't caring about Negroes. And now some child is going to judge me?

SMINTHEUS: It's just a question of morality.

KARL: It's a question of survival, my friend. (*Pause.*)

[33]

Look, do you want to know why I married a white woman?

[They respond with silence.]

LENA: (*finally jumping up, teasingly*) Yes, yes, we're all dying to know why you married a white woman!

[They laugh.]

KARL: All right. I simply got tired of having doors slammed in my face all the time. I got tired of not getting the apartment I wanted. I got tired of having taxicabs leave me behind on street corners. I married someone who wouldn't be a hindrance to my career. Someone to deal with all the amenities of the society, the smiles, the name-dropping, and all the rest.

SMINTHEUS: You were programmed.

KARL: No, I wasn't, I made the choice. I had tried both worlds and found them wanting. (*Pause.*) And of course I love her.

[They all look at Karl for a full second.]

LENA: (*breaking the silence*) So I see you're writing a book, Smintheus.

SMINTHEUS: Yes.

LENA: How nice.

[Darkness.]

Scene 5

[Smintheus is seated at a table in what appears to be a jazz club. A very sexy black girl comes over to his table. She is bold yet very shy. She covers her mouth when she laughs because she has poor teeth. She is a prostitute and wears a stereotyped red dress.]

MARGIE: Hi.

SMINTHEUS: (*fiddling with his drink*) Hi. Hi. Hi. Hi.

MARGIE: (*sitting down beside him*) They really sound good, don't they?

SMINTHEUS: Yes, quite adequate—I mean. . . . (*Pause.*) Good sound.

MARGIE: I like jazz . . . I mean I really dig jazz. You know, I could hear it all the time.

SMINTHEUS: Oh.

MARGIE: I'm Margie.

SMINTHEUS: How fortunate for you.

MARGIE: You're a lawyer, right?

SMINTHEUS: How could you tell, Margie?

MARGIE: You have a nice fat face. Your eyes are kind of baggy. You got a distinguished bald spot in the middle of your head.

SMINTHEUS: Oh.

MARGIE: Very . . . you know, distinguished. (*She makes a few pointless motions with her hand.*) Distinguished.

SMINTHEUS: Would you like a drink, Margie?

MARGIE: I wouldn't refuse. (*Laughing.*) You know.

SMINTHEUS: What would you like? Champagne?

MARGIE: Champagne. Yes, man, for days. Champagne?

SMINTHEUS: (*signaling the waiter*) A bottle of your best champagne for pretty Margie and the lawyer.

MARGIE: Heh heh.

SMINTHEUS: Why are you laughing?

MARGIE: Because I feel good.

SMINTHEUS: Oh, then you should laugh.

[*Drinks are brought over. Smintheus pays the waiter.*]

MARGIE: I don't remember seeing you in Minton's before.

SMINTHEUS: Oh, I've been here before. Do you know Grace?

MARGIE: Grace Tyner, the light-skin chick who used to work here?

SMINTHEUS: Yeah. Did she quit?

MARGIE: Oh, Grace, she canceled.

SMINTHEUS: Canceled?

MARGIE: She's dead, man.

SMINTHEUS: Dead?

MARGIE: Yeah, dead, as in—you know—dead.

SMINTHEUS: Dead from what?

MARGIE: I think they said pneumonia. It doesn't matter, she's dead, you know.

SMINTHEUS: Yes, I guess you're right. Well, here's to Margie's dress.

MARGIE: My dress. (*Pause.*) OK, yeah, that's hip.

SMINTHEUS: (*slyly*) Whatever do you do, Margie?

MARGIE: Do? I move around, you know.

SMINTHEUS: Oh.

MARGIE: Are you really a lawyer?

SMINTHEUS: No.

MARGIE: What do you do?

SMINTHEUS: I'm a sociologist. (*Pause.*) I think.

MARGIE: Sociologist, wow, that's far-out. (*Pause.*) What does a sociologist do?

SMINTHEUS: Nothing.

MARGIE: Oh. You're very bright, right?

SMINTHEUS: If memory serves right, yeah.

MARGIE: You look like a lawyer.

SMINTHEUS: Thanks.

MARGIE: You want to cop some stuff?

SMINTHEUS: No, I think not.

MARGIE: You don't?

SMINTHEUS: No. (*Pause.*) I'd like to have you, though.

MARGIE: Oh yeah, well, I hear you talking.

SMINTHEUS: You say I'm going bald, eh?

MARGIE: Well, it's not all that bad but it's going, you know. Why, it really upsets you, eh?

SMINTHEUS: No. No.

MARGIE: You're really weird; what's your sign?

SMINTHEUS: My sign?

MARGIE: Astrology sign.

SMINTHEUS: Scorpio, I think.

MARGIE: Yeah, yeah, a Scorpio, that's right, it makes sense.

SMINTHEUS: Is that good?

MARGIE: Yeah, it's all right, you know. (*Pause.*) You want to cop some ups?

SMINTHEUS: No, no ups, thank you. Just you. I'd really . . . like to do all sorts of indelicate things with you, Margie.

MARGIE: Damn, you talk more shit than the radio.

SMINTHEUS: I think I should tell you I'm a married man, Margie.

MARGIE: Well, that ain't no big thing. I don't really want to marry you.

SMINTHEUS: Bells. Bells. Bells. Bells. Ding, ding, ding, ding, dong, ding.

MARGIE: What?

SMINTHEUS: Every now and then I think I'm a bell.

MARGIE: A bell? What do you want to be a bell for?

SMINTHEUS: Go ding-dong in the morning.

MARGIE: Ding-dong? Yeah, I could dig that. Why do you wear that flower in your lapel?

SMINTHEUS: It's Richard Wagner's birthday.

MARGIE: Whose birthday?

SMINTHEUS: It's not important, Margie. Take me home.

MARGIE: I don't know.

SMINTHEUS: Why? I won't tell anyone.

MARGIE: Ha-ha, I don't care if you tell anyone, fool. I'm just wondering if you're a cop. You're a little too weird.

SMINTHEUS: Cop? Me cop? Me no cop. Me Smintheus, the sociologist. You girl. Me like girl very much. Me wantum eat up girl.

MARGIE: (*laughing, covering her mouth*) Did you really think I'd mind if you told anybody?

SMINTHEUS: Well, I didn't want you to think I was one of those fellows.

MARGIE: Ha-ha. What?

SMINTHEUS: Nothing.

MARGIE: Come on (*rising*).

SMINTHEUS: (*going after her, looking at her in her red dress*) Oh, my God. (*He leaves tip and exits.*)

[*Darkness.*]

Scene 6

[*The two Dwarfs cross the stage again, carrying a sign reading: "Smintheus Loses His Ding-Dong."*

The scene again includes the prison background. Smintheus is writing to Robert.]

SMINTHEUS: "Dear Robert, All is not well with me. Several days ago I met a girl at Minton's. She was a cute little Harlem thing and really quite delicious. However, I seem to have contracted a rather quaint disease of the genitals. I was afraid it was the clap. However, yesterday the doctor informed me that I had syphilis. All of which is really quite exciting except that I have had to inform Joyce. I thought her response excessive. She hurled several heavy objects toward me with the intention of doing me harm. I don't believe the girl involved (her name is Margie) meant to give me this ailment willfully. I'm sure she doesn't know that she has it. I'm sure there is something to be learned from the experience although I don't quite know what. Well, these things and others are among my disquietudes.

"I heard John Coltrane the other day. I found his musicianship adequate, although I don't quite understand what direction he's heading toward. Almost finished with the third volume. I'm trying to find a way of using Morgenstern's Zero Sum game theory in my analysis of the American Negro and the competitive system. At the same time I must be careful not to make it seem like Marxist dialectics or something. You should be out in a few months. That will be good: we have lots to do. I haven't been sleeping much lately. I'm more on edge than usual. It will be over soon though. Yours, J. Walter."

ROBERT: "Dear Idiot, Do you mean to tell me you let yourself get burned by some whore? I didn't think you were so stupid. I mean I knew you were stupid but I didn't think you were that stupid. Well, anyway, keep working. She's only a woman after all. You'll be dead and she'll be dead but the work will exist later on when it's important.

"I don't know how much help I'll be to you when I get out. They've just about killed anything I had. I've tried to do some writing but my mind is too confused in this place. I'm so busy trying to keep these people from making a faggot out of me. (They'll probably censor this letter although they've been letting most of my letters get past.) It must mean that they don't think I'm a threat anymore. When they stop censoring your letters that means they think you're going crazy.

"Keep working and don't forget that definition you gave me in that sociology class: 'Man is a featherless biped that marries on occasion.' Yours, Robert."

[Darkness.]

Scene 7

[Smintheus is at home, seated in his rocking chair. He is covered with a carpet. His wife enters the room. Smintheus has an open book in his lap. He has fallen asleep. She takes the book, places a marker between the pages, and closes it. His face is haggard, with beard and baggy eyes.]

JOYCE: Smintheus, I want to speak to you.

[No response.]

Smintheus.

SMINTHEUS: Hmm . . . ah . . . Joyce . . . I must have . . . um . . .

JOYCE: Smintheus, I can't take this anymore. I've tried but I can't anymore.

SMINTHEUS: Joyce . . .

JOYCE: Smintheus, for four years now I have been married to a walking library.

SMINTHEUS: Joyce, I . . . understand that life . . . that our life has been somewhat trying.

JOYCE: (*pausing coyly*) Yeah, somewhat trying, Smintheus. You know when I met you I was . . . well, I guess I was intrigued by your tweed jackets and your pipe tobacco and your way of speaking.

SMINTHEUS: Joyce . . .

JOYCE: Well, it's not happening anymore. I am sick and tired of having my husband for an hour a day. I am sick and tired of having sex twice on the weekend.

SMINTHEUS: Well, Joyce, I believe we've had more than that.

JOYCE: Yeah, there've been moments when you've had flushes of passion. Then you'd come running in and rape me in the middle of whatever I was doing. But that's not what marriage is about. You just sit in here in your goddamn rocking chair.

SMINTHEUS: Now Joyce, please. I'm not up to this today. I . . .

JOYCE: And what the hell are you doing with that carpet around you?

SMINTHEUS: I was a bit chilly.

JOYCE: It's June.

SMINTHEUS: I was still a bit chilly; must be a draft coming from somewhere (*looking around him for draft*).

JOYCE: You just sit in here and write that junkie jailbird friend of yours.

SMINTHEUS: Joyce, that's not nice.

JOYCE: You look like some kind of a . . . an owl. Your eyes are sticking out of your head. You haven't changed your clothes in a month. You haven't shaved, you stink. The room is filled with smoke. Why don't you ever let some air in here?

SMINTHEUS: Too much smog outside.

JOYCE: Well, listen, it's just not happening anymore.

SMINTHEUS: What's not happening anymore?

JOYCE: There's just nothing—absolutely nothing except that I'm hating you more every day. (*Pause.*) Do you know what my parents would do to you if they ever found out that you gave me syphilis? You took me out of Philadelphia to give me syphilis!

SMINTHEUS: I didn't give you syphilis willfully. And you've been to the doctor; it was just a mild . . .

JOYCE: OK. All right. All men play around to a certain extent, but you would think that you would at least have the decency to go with civilized women.

[44]

SMINTHEUS: Joyce, can't we . . .

JOYCE: No, we can't. I can't make it anymore. It's too much for any woman. I could have married a lawyer or . . . or a doctor from Howard University or something. There were plenty of them who were interested. Instead I've got . . . a rocking chair. You know that book will never get done?

SMINTHEUS: All right, Joyce. What do you want?

JOYCE: It's called a divorce.

SMINTHEUS: A divorce?

JOYCE: It's very respectable; even white people do it.

SMINTHEUS: I know *they* do it.

JOYCE: Well, it's time that I did it.

SMINTHEUS: Joyce, I don't have the time for a divorce.

JOYCE: I have a good lawyer. He says we can do the whole thing in a week.

SMINTHEUS: A week. This is an age of speed, isn't it? Joyce (*in mock solicitation*), who's going to do my typing for me?

JOYCE: Get a typist, you bastard!

SMINTHEUS: (*taking her in his arms*) Joyce, why don't we . . .

JOYCE: No. (*She pushes him away.*) Did you ever love

me? Did you ever love anybody except the Society of Arts and Letters?

SMINTHEUS: Well . . . I like the way your arm looks on top of the sheets in the morning. It's a very thin arm but I like it. And after four years of marriage you still look good to me naked. That's whatever . . . love is, I think.

JOYCE: Got to do better than that.

> *[The telephone rings. Joyce walks to the phone and answers.]*

Hello . . . who? Who is this? What? (*She rests the phone on her breast and looks at Smintheus coyly.*) It's for you, dear.

SMINTHEUS: Me?

JOYCE: Yes, it's your mistress, Margie. (*She hands him the phone.*)

SMINTHEUS: Er . . . Joyce.

> *[She looks at him and leaves.]*

Hello, Margie . . . you really called at a most inopportune time. What? What's the matter—are you crying? You're drunk? You're not drunk? You're a little drunk? Margie, how did you get my telephone number? My wallet? Margie, do you know that you gave me syphilis? I know you're sorry, Margie. Listen, why don't you . . . Margie, please . . . Margie. (*He drops the phone and goes to approach Joyce.*)

> *[She looks at him. He takes her hand; her fingers are arched like claws. She thinks about scratching his*

face, decides not to. She turns to go, thinks again, and turns and slaps him. Then she exits. He puts his hand to his head. Margie's voice can be heard on the phone, calling him. He slowly walks back to the phone, picks up the receiver and speaks.]

Yes, Margie. Margie, my wife has just left me. No, Margie, I don't hate you. . . . Stop crying . . . no, I do not love you . . . I don't . . . I can't love anybody more than anybody, I . . . Margie, don't say that. . . . Because it's not nice to go around calling people a motherfucker. . . . All right . . . if you say so that's what I am. Listen, why don't you sober up and . . . no, no, Margie, I, well . . . where are you? You're in a telephone booth? What telephone booth, Margie? What street are you? . . . You don't know? Well, how can you know? . . . All right, take a taxi to my house. It's Lenox Terrace Apartments on 135th and . . . yes, all right, I'll pay him once he gets here. Just take a taxi . . . any taxi. I'll . . .

[Darkness.]

Scene 8

[Smintheus is seated in his rocking chair. He hears the bell and rises, goes to the door. Enter Margie and haggard-looking white male friend of hers. He looks like an unsuccessful bohemian. Margie is dressed in slacks and a blouse. She has an Afro.]

SMINTHEUS: Margie, I was wondering what happened to you. You phoned five hours ago.

MARGIE: I got lost. May I have a drink?

SMINTHEUS: Yes. I believe . . . yeah, there's some brandy on that bookcase.

BOB: Margie says you blow sax.

MARGIE: I said he was a sociologist, not a saxophonist.

BOB: Damn it, sounded like you said saxophonist. Yeah, okay. I used to blow a horn. (*He pours a drink.*)

SMINTHEUS: How does one go about becoming an ex-musician?

BOB: It's easy, man. You just stop. (*He sits in the rocking chair.*)

SMINTHEUS: Margie . . . I don't really feel like entertaining.

MARGIE: Wow, Smintheus. So many books and paintings.

SMINTHEUS: *The Negro Encyclopedia,* several volumes of the poetry of James Weldon Johnson, African *objet d'art* facing African *objet d'art.* Autographed copy of Du Bois's *Souls of Black Folk.* Picture of Catherine Jarboro, first Negro prima donna. Autographed copy of Ralph Ellison's *Invisible Man.* History of African and Hawaiian folklore. The original manuscripts of William Stills's Afro-American Symphony. Three paintings of Charles White. Two maps of Ghana. Joyce's collected issues of *Reader's Digest* and *Ebony.*

MARGIE: You make it all sound pretty boring.

SMINTHEUS: It is.

[Bob slumps over in his chair and falls asleep.]

MARGIE: Oh, wow.

SMINTHEUS: (*pointing to Bob*) Who . . . ?

MARGIE: His name is Bob Kaufman. I ran into him at Slug's. He's not very together but he's all right. His parents messed him up. They're rich or something.

SMINTHEUS: *He's* not together? Whatever possessed you to call me at my house?

MARGIE: Man, I was so stoned. I don't even remember calling you except that I wrote your address down.

SMINTHEUS: Margie, do you know my wife left me?

MARGIE: Yeah, I'm sorry. But look, I'll take care of you. I mean, I don't dig cooking and all of that too tough, but you know I could get it together . . . for a while, you know. You could meet my son.

SMINTHEUS: Your son?

MARGIE: Yeah, I got a little boy eight years old. You'd like him. He's just like you, digs books and like that. He stays with my grandmother . . . does real good in school.

SMINTHEUS: You have a son eight years old?

MARGIE: Uh huh. Ahem . . . the doctor says I can't have

any sex for at least a month. Got to keep taking penicillin shots but I'll be better soon.

SMINTHEUS: And what will we do for a month, Joyce?

MARGIE: I'm Margie.

SMINTHEUS: I'm sorry.

MARGIE: (*caressing him*) I'll find some way to keep you happy. Is that your wife in that picture?

SMINTHEUS: Yes, that's Joyce and the gentleman with the insipid grin on his face is myself on the occasion of my marriage.

MARGIE: She's very pretty.

SMINTHEUS: Yes, here's another one that appeared in the *Pittsburgh Courier.*

MARGIE: (*reading*) "Miss Joyce Thompson, daughter of the prominent Philadelphia perfumer, Horace Thompson, weds J. Walter Smintheus, the son of Edmund Smintheus, the Atlanta funeral director. Mr. Smintheus is a *cum laude* graduate of Cornell University."

SMINTHEUS: Yes, very exciting.

MARGIE: This another one of her?

SMINTHEUS: Yes, that's Joyce standing next to a half-naked limbo dancer in the Bahamas.

MARGIE: Why did she pose next to the half-naked limbo dancer?

SMINTHEUS: I suppose because she wanted to.

MARGIE: Oh.

SMINTHEUS: Margie, I don't think—

MARGIE: Shhhh. Do you like me?

SMINTHEUS: Yes . . . I—

MARGIE: I like you too; we'll help each other.

[*End in bed. Darkness. Satie music starts up.*]

Scene 9

[*Smintheus's nightmare: In this dream sequence, Smintheus and his wife, both fashionably dressed, make an entrance into a high-society restaurant, Hagia Sophia; this name is on the wall above the table at which Smintheus is attempting to be seated. Smintheus walks in and is approached by the Waiter. There are three white couples circumscribing Smintheus.*]

SMINTHEUS: Ah, there are our seats over there, Joyce.

WAITER: (*cutting across*) Yes. What is it?

SMINTHEUS: I made arrangements for two, Paul.

WAITER: Arrangements? Do you mean reservations, sir?

SMINTHEUS: Yes, of course, reservations.

WAITER: What is your name, sir?

SMINTHEUS: My name is Smintheus, of course, Paul. I've been eating here for three years.

WAITER: For three years. I'm sorry, sir, but I've never seen you before and there were no reservations made.

SMINTHEUS: What are you talking about? I called yesterday. Paul, what's wrong with you?

[*The three couples stare at Smintheus.*]

WAITER: I don't know how you know my name, but I assure you there's nothing wrong with me.

MANAGER: (*coming over*) What seems to be the problem here?

JOYCE: What's wrong with them, Smintheus?

WAITER: Sir, this man is implying there is something wrong with me.

MANAGER: Why do you say these unkind things about my nephew?

WAITER: He wants to hurt me.

SMINTHEUS: I meant to imply nothing.

MANAGER: Have you medical evidence to support your allegations? Some means of proving that there is indeed something wrong with my nephew?

SMINTHEUS: Well, I'll tell you, when I have been coming to a restaurant regularly for three years and call in to make reservations, only to have the same waiter tell me he's never seen me before and that I made no reservation, I'm forced to wonder if something is wrong with him.

MANAGER: (*with utter suspicion*) Say, aren't you colored?

SMINTHEUS: (*looking at Joyce*) Yes, yes, I'm colored, whatever that means.

[*The crowd turns again.*]

MANAGER: Are you drunk?

SMINTHEUS: No.

MANAGER: Are you sure?

SMINTHEUS: (*pausing*) Yes, I'm sure.

MANAGER: Is he for real?

SMINTHEUS: (*looking at Joyce*) Yes, I'm real.

MANAGER: Do you know what restaurant this is?

SMINTHEUS: Yes.

JOYCE: Smintheus, we don't have to take this.

MANAGER: Which is it?

SMINTHEUS: It's Hagia Sophia.

WAITER: He has a speech impediment. Say nuncle me no nuncle.

SMINTHEUS: Nuncle me no nuncle.

MANAGER: (*to the Waiter*) It's not too bad.

SMINTHEUS: Listen, I want to know what's going on.

MANAGER: What's going on?

SMINTHEUS: Yes, I have the right to know.

MANAGER: Have you always been colored?

SMINTHEUS: Yes, as long as I can remember.

MANAGER: And you say we let you eat here.

SMINTHEUS: I've been eating here for three years.

MANAGER: Have you any calling cards?

SMINTHEUS: Calling cards?

MANAGER: Private calling cards, you twit. Something to represent you?

SMINTHEUS: (*fumbling in his pocket*) I have some credit cards . . . somewhere . . . ah, here they are. (*He presents the cards.*)

MANAGER: Let's see.

[*The Waiter looks over the Manager's shoulder.*]

Smintheus, eh?

SMINTHEUS: Yes, Smintheus.

JOYCE: Smintheus, if you don't take me out of here this second . . .

MANAGER: This one says Cornell. Did you attend Cornell?

SMINTHEUS: Yes. (*Proudly.*) Class of . . .

MANAGER: Sports, eh?

SMINTHEUS: No, sociology.

MANAGER: Are you a musician?

SMINTHEUS: No, a sociologist.

MANAGER: Too bad; it would have been easier to take you if you were a musician. (*To the Waiter.*) Is anyone sitting here, Paul? (*He gives Smintheus his credit cards.*)

WAITER: (*staring at the vacant table*) No, sir.

MANAGER: All right, let them sit there while I speak to Chef Le Dieu. He may quit if he has to cook for you. Give them the *tarnished* set of silverware and a wine list. (*To Smintheus.*) Better give me back those credit cards; I'll show them to him. It may do some good.

[*Smintheus gives him back the cards.*]

What's this? (*He looks in Smintheus's wallet and sees a playing card.*) The ace of spades.

SMINTHEUS: Yes.

JOYCE: Smintheus, I told you to throw that away.

MANAGER: Why do you keep it in your wallet?

[55]

SMINTHEUS: I thought it was amusing.

MANAGER: (*looking at Smintheus, incredulously*) Keep an eye on them, Paul. (*He exits.*)

JOYCE: Smintheus, why don't we leave?

SMINTHEUS: If we did that, we would seem guilty. We must never seem guilty. (*Seating Joyce first and then himself. Pause.*) Oh, Joyce, I just thought of that word in the crossword puzzle.

JOYCE: What word?

SMINTHEUS: The word in the crossword puzzle. A six-letter word for animals without a nervous system.

MANAGER: Let me see your hands.

[Smintheus presents the palms of his hands.]

All right, now the backs. What's that blue stain between your fingers?

SMINTHEUS: I'm a writer. It's probably ink from a pen.

MANAGER: All right. (*To Joyce.*) You now.

[She shows her hands reluctantly.]

Now the backs. All right. That's a beautiful ring. Is it real?

JOYCE: (*indignantly*) I shan't even answer that.

MANAGER: All right. (*He exits.*)

[56]

JOYCE: What is the word?

SMINTHEUS: What word?

JOYCE: The word for animals without a nervous system?

SMINTHEUS: Oh, acrita.

JOYCE: Oh.

SMINTHEUS: Strange, that I shouldn't have remembered it. I was very good in biology.

JOYCE: Smintheus.

SMINTHEUS: Yes, Joyce.

JOYCE: Do you love me, Smintheus?

SMINTHEUS: Yes, and very much.

MANAGER: (*reentering*) Le Dieu wants you described.

SMINTHEUS: Described?

MANAGER: Yes. Would you call yourself very dark?

SMINTHEUS: Not very.

JOYCE: Smintheus, I would be described as light. You are considerably darker than me; therefore you would be described as dark.

SMINTHEUS: All right, Joyce. Yes, I'm dark.

MANAGER: (*writing everything down*) Your lips are

thick, Negroid. Your expession is sort of simplistic. Yes, that would be the best way to say it. Stand up, please.

[Smintheus rises.]

You're above average size. (*He takes a quick glimpse at Smintheus's trousers.*) Probably oversexed. Buttocks over-large. (*He goes over to Joyce.*)

JOYCE: (*exasperated*) Oh, really. (*She, too, rises.*)

MANAGER: Ah. Not overly bovine in figure. Nice legs.

SMINTHEUS: That's from playing tennis.

MANAGER: Oh, really, do you play tennis?

SMINTHEUS: She has a wicked backhand.

MANAGER: (*writing*) Wicked backhand, very interesting. Say, you aren't that tennis-playing Negro woman . . .

JOYCE: No, that's not me.

MANAGER: Pity, it would have eased matters considerably.

[Meals are being brought to various tables.]

SMINTHEUS: Excuse me, but we are very hungry.

MANAGER: (*angrily*) Yes, yes, I'll take this back to Le Dieu. He's afraid that your taste facilities have been dulled by excessive amounts of pork.

SMINTHEUS: That's absurd. I've been eating here for three years.

MANAGER: All right, all right. I'll tell him. (*He turns to the other customers.*) Please forgive this intrusion. It will all be cleared up soon. Feel perfectly safe, they won't harm you. He attended Cornell. She plays tennis. (*He exits.*)

[*Mozart is heard from a speaker.*]

SMINTHEUS: Ah, Joyce, Mozart.

[*One of the diners, a portly fellow, gets up and comes over to their table.*]

DINER: Excuse me, but that is Chopin, not Mozart.

SMINTHEUS: I beg your pardon, but that's Mozart.

DINER: (*turning to the others*) Do you hear that! He's going to tell us about our music.

SMINTHEUS: I only said that . . .

DINER: How would you know what it is? It doesn't have any drums in it.

[*Everyone laughs.*]

DINER: (*seating himself again*) Mozart.

JOYCE: Smintheus, that's it! I won't stay here another minute.

SMINTHEUS: Joyce, it must be some kind of game. They all know me; they're just having a little fun, I guess.

MANAGER: (*reentering*) Le Dieu would like to know what your average was at Cornell.

SMINTHEUS: You know, this game is growing tedious. You've all ceased to be amusing.

MANAGER: What was your . . .

SMINTHEUS: I had an A average.

MANAGER: Did you graduate?

SMINTHEUS: *Cum laude.*

MANAGER: (*making a motion as if to go, then turning back*) And you weren't an athlete?

JOYCE: Smintheus, why should they suddenly want to play such games?

SMINTHEUS: I don't know.

JOYCE: When he comes back, choke him and see what he does.

SMINTHEUS: I think it would be better to act perfectly normal.

JOYCE: Perfectly normal? How?

SMINTHEUS: (*looking at the wine list*) What's this? Waiter.

[*The Waiter comes over.*]

This is no wine list, it's in Greek.

WAITER: What? Oh, I'm terribly sorry. I don't know how that got there. Here. I'll get you another.

SMINTHEUS: It's all right, Paul. Just get me a light German wine.

WAITER: I don't know if Le Dieu will approve.

SMINTHEUS: It's all right. Just tell him to remember those in sorrow, sickness, and need.

WAITER: Sorrow, sickness, I'll tell him. (*He exits.*)

JOYCE: Please! Let's leave, Smintheus. I think everyone's gone crazy. I'm frightened.

SMINTHEUS: Don't worry, it will all work out somehow, I'm sure.

JOYCE: You act as if you always expected this to happen.

SMINTHEUS: Don't worry.

MANAGER: (*entering hurriedly*) I'm sorry, it's no good. You'll have to leave. Here—take your credit cards. Le Dieu says no.

SMINTHEUS: Come along, Joyce.

MANAGER: I'm sorry, but you do see our predicament?

SMINTHEUS: (*leaving, turning, and smiling uncomfortably*) It is Mozart. (*He leaves a ten-dollar tip.*)

MANAGER: (*to the Waiter*) Burn the silverware.

[Darkness.]

Scene 10

[Smintheus and Margie. Margie is asleep in Smintheus's arms as the scene opens. He tries to wake her, taps her softly several times on the head. No response.]

SMINTHEUS: Margie . . . too late. (*He looks around him.*) It's early. Wake up now . . . come on. She's going to support me. (*He looks at her neck.*) You have very strong neck muscles. Healthy little creature. You don't understand, do you? You don't understand what I mean when I say I'm running out of certainties. You don't understand what I mean when I say my heart (*pause*) or is it my mind . . . is in sad disrepair. The music that you like to listen to hurts me too much. Perhaps you like it because it hurts you. But it hurts me too much. Even your eyes . . . the implications of your eyes hurt me too much. I wish there were some way to learn about this world safely. I wish it didn't cost so much. I think you learned too much, too. You're a little too well acquainted with pain. Maybe we could just slow time down a bit. Drink coffee and eat cake. Go out to dinner twice a week. Develop an interest in television. Have you read to me in the bathtub. . . . (*Long pause; he looks at her.*) I wonder why you're not as frightened as I am.

[Darkness.]

Scene 11

[Smintheus is seated at his desk, writing a letter to Robert. He is a solitary figure this time.]

SMINTHEUS: "Dear Robert, My coffee has not been prepared and I haven't heard any noises in the bathroom, which must mean that Joyce has left me. I think I miss her. Margie has suggested living with me, but I don't think I feel like having any woman right now. I have been neglectful of my toilet and remiss in my dress of late. Everything seems to be happening so quickly I don't know what's going on. The work is growing more difficult all the time. I've been making a lot of reference to E. Franklin Frazier and Fanon. I don't quite know where to go from here. . . ."

[The telephone rings several times before Smintheus finally hears it. He looks around him for a while, bewildered. He then goes down on his knees along the floor and follows the telephone wire through the morass of papers and books. He finally locates the phone and speaks.]

Hello, I'm sorry I took so long to answer but it seems as though my wife has left me and the house is in a bit of disorder. Who is this? Bob's what? Oh, Robert's sister? He never mentioned he had a sister. I'm just writing to him. What? Oh, don't cry now. Everybody cries on the phone these days. What happened? He did what? What do you mean, "OD"? Overdose of what? Heroin? But he's gone to prison—he can't get . . . he can get drugs in prison? But he can't be dead. . . . (*He drops the phone in a trancelike state and continues the conversation while walking about, as if still speaking on the phone.*) No, no, he can't be dead. You see, it's in five volumes. We have to get together and, well . . . he's my friend; he can't die forever. I mean, I would be alone then. And have to take them on by myself. I mean, well, if . . . I mean . . . he can't just die because we have so much . . . and we were going to take a trip to the Bahamas so he could rest up and then we would begin the last two . . . well, I mean . . . he can't have just . . .

[Darkness.]

Scene 12

[Smintheus is seated in the sanitarium of the opening scene. He is facing the audience in his rocking chair. Another patient (who should be played by a dancer) slithers into his room, crawling on his hands, one leg resting upon another, in the manner of a paralytic. When he comes to the rocking chair, he turns and looks at the audience. His mouth is contorted, his leg in a backward and unnatural position, as patients sometimes sit when in a catatonic state. The recorded voice of Smintheus is again heard.]

SMINTHEUS: Because it must have been winter then. And I was walking along some sort of street, and the snow had covered everything. No cars moved and the snow was so bright. But where could I have been that there was so much snow and silence? No one knows. I saw no one else walking. But where could I have been that there was so much silence?

It was so cold: I didn't think it could be so cold anywhere. And there was a statue of a boy—seated, with his legs crossed. And I remember thinking that I should not forget this boy because he was important in some way. But what reference could he have had to anything in my life? And my shadow was growing on the snow, and that frightened me then. But what could the dead boy have to do with my life? And then there were those mice running out from beneath damp rocks.

It's very peaceful here. The music will come soon. Perhaps if I learned my name they would leave me alone. I'll just sit here something like this and watch the stars break up on the floor. (*Pause.*)

[*Darkness.*]

The Crucificado

To Albert Leveau, who saw it through, Uyi Efeoubokham and Gilbert Moses

Characters

MOROSE, *architect-writer*
SOLEDADA, *lover of Morose*
CELESTINA (*or* YVONNE), *lover of Morose*
EL CID, *Morose's father*
CHORUS:
   GONGORA, *a blind man*
   PEDRO (*or* PAUL), *thin like a flame*
   RAFAEL, *a West Indian*
MELIBEA, *niece of El Cid and mulatto*
LA PASIONARIA, *Puerto Rican drug dealer*

THE CRUCIFICADO was first performed at Vinnette Carroll's Urban Arts Corps in June, 1972. It was directed by Darryl Hill.

Cast members and their roles are as follows:

MOROSE	DARRYL HILL
SOLEDADA	DEAN RADCLIFF
CELESTINA	ROSEMARY STEWART
EL CID	VANCE WILLIAMS
GONGORA	CARMA
PEDRO	KEITH BURNS
RAFAEL	ANDY JOHNSON

MELIBEA   LINDA DARLING

LA PASIONARIA   COLETTE HILL

Author's note:

The play is a very free one. The movement will determine the form. There are vast spaces in which improvisation can be done. To play a drama the same way each time is death.

The character Morose, however, must be played with the fluctuations in mood that connote his irony. The names of the characters Pedro and Celestina may be changed to Paul and Yvonne if the director so chooses. The play may be done either with black or Spanish actors.

The play takes place on a polyscenic stage in which many different small stages are used. The action of the play is continuous.

Scene 1

Dream Sequence

[*Morose rises from bed, where he was lying asleep beside Soledada. He walks toward that section of stage which is to be Street. He encounters La Pasionaria, the Puerto Rican girl who deals him dope. There are two thin, pinlike posts crosswise with pearl heads; they will represent the church. Throughout the play the actors make use of this. At the end Morose should exit toward these pins. Yellow and green lights for this dream sequence. Music by Bobby Hutcherson and Sam Rivers: "Dialogue."*]

MOROSE: (*moving like a Kung Fu master, graceful, as a junkie's dream should be. Recorded voice of Morose*)

> I know I'm going to find him,
> see him close in his face.
> There'll be some peace then
> streets won't be so damp.

LA PASIONARIA: Hey, Morose, what you into? Got something for you.

MOROSE: Can't stop now. Got to find Death, he's been messing with Little Sister. She ain't even got breasts yet, she looks like a wall.

LA PASIONARIA: Want to get high? I know you want to get high. I got something to make the tip of your dick burn.

MOROSE: No, can't stop now. Distractions in your eyes but I got to find Death.

LA PASIONARIA: You going look for him in that church. Death ain't in no church. What you doing, you going to make novena or something? (*She exits on this line, her back to him.*) Death ain't in no church.

MOROSE: (*going up to cross-pins*) The doors are locked. Damn, how could they lock the doors of a church? La Pasionaria, the doors are locked. They all locked. (*He returns to bed.*)

[*Chorus enters.*]

[*Darkness.*]

Scene 2

[*The scene opens with the full chorus of the three beggars. Gongora reveals himself first. He is led in by Pedro. Gongora's cane opens to a little chair which he sits upon.*]

GONGORA: *Voces de sangre y sangre del alma.* . . . What is the occasion and why have we come here? Is it to sing of the fall of some great man, a man alone among many men?

PEDRO: We rest here because I'm tired, old man. All day long I have to lead your ass around, I'm tired now.

RAFAEL: Nothing to drink.

GONGORA: Let me park myself here along the edge of time.

PEDRO: Oh shit, there he goes again. The prophet Gongora (*with genuine disgust*).

GONGORA: (*reaches inside his shirt and withdraws some cheese, wrapped in a cloth, which he absentmindedly begins eating*) Did I hear someone screaming? (*Lifts head.*) It sounded like a young girl.

RAFAEL: That must have been the sound of Pedro farting.

[*The two of them laugh.*]

[*Darkness.*]

[*The Chorus is to stage right. They are seated and staring with great bemusement at the lone figure of Morose on stage center. He is seated at a table. He pours three glasses of Scotch. Very meticulously. Then calls to offstage.*]

MOROSE: Soledada. (*Silence.*) Soledada. (*Long pause.*) Lazy little bitch.

SOLEDADA: (*entering*) Were you speaking to me, Morose?

MOROSE: No, of course not, sweetheart. Just sitting here speaking to myself. Soledada, fetch me my calmative, please.

SOLEDADA: Do you mean your dope?

MOROSE: Yes, of course I mean my dope. It's morning, isn't it? What else would I be calling for?

SOLEDADA: (*She moves her young, light-skinned, black-bourgeoise body across the stage to a small table at stage left and removes from drawer, a nefarious-looking, brown-paper bag. Returns and lays it down in front of Morose.*) I wish you didn't use this.

MOROSE: No, what you mean is that you wish I didn't need this. However (*long pause wherein he takes a nail file and snorts two large mounds of heroin*), so happens that I do.

SOLEDADA: I just wish you didn't have this problem.

MOROSE: No problem, honey, as long as I get my thing. The world got a problem. (*He drinks down the first glass of Scotch.*)

SOLEDADA: And then alcohol on top of the dope. That's really not good for you.

MOROSE: Honey, life is not good for you. Did anyone ever tell you that?

SOLEDADA: Yes—you did. You can play all the games you want to, that stuff is going to destroy you.

MOROSE: Goddammit, bitch. You need air to breathe, don't you? Well, I need this motherfucker to live. To live, you understand. Now I don't ever want to talk about it agin.

[Soledada walks away. She seems hurt. He pauses a

moment; continues to get high. Pinpoints where he is standing. Then he says in low voice]

Listen, dope is just one of the things I love. For example, I love your ass. In fact, I love you. I love music, thinking . . . (*Becomes very peaceful now; the dope is working.*) What else I love . . . something else?

SOLEDADA: Yes, except this one thing happens to be the one that's going to kill you.

MOROSE: Sometimes it causes you nothing less than your life to live, you know what I mean?

SOLEDADA: It would be such a waste to lose you.

MOROSE: Lose me, lose me, who's going to lose me? Just let me make sure that I don't lose me.

[She sits down in his lap.]

SOLEDADA: (*very childishly*) You have some on the side of your nose.

MOROSE: You lucky bitch.

SOLEDADA: Why am I lucky?

[Morose points to himself three times.]

Don't tell me. Because I have you, right?

MOROSE: Right.

SOLEDADA: (*looks to heaven*) Thank you, Jesus, for sending me a junkie for a boyfriend.

MOROSE: I wish you wouldn't use that word.

SOLEDADA: You mean *junkie.* (*She says the word with especial melodrama.*)

MOROSE: Oh, I don't give a fuck if you call me a junkie. Just don't be calling me your boyfriend. It smells like pretzels.

SOLEDADA: What do pretzels smell like?

MOROSE: Like your mama. Listen, don't you have some woman business to attend to?

SOLEDADA: You mean like supporting you?

MOROSE: Yes, I mean like supporting us. Get thee to the sulfur mine, woman.

SOLEDADA: (*looking at watch*) You're right, it's almost nine-thirty. Listen, don't forget to take the clothes to the laundry.

MOROSE: (*mimicking her*) I won't forget to take the clothes to the laundry.

SOLEDADA: Listen, if I was home all day. . . . (*Pause. Decides against saying any more.*)

MOROSE: Come here.

[*Soledada goes to the other side of stage and gathers up pocketbook and a little looseleaf pad.*]

Come here, I said. (*Reaches out for her and kisses her on her behind.*) I love you very much.

SOLEDADA: So what? . . .

MOROSE: Shh. The few hours of my life that I have enjoyed have been with you and heroin.

SOLEDADA: Suppose you had to make a choice?

MOROSE: I'd pass.

SOLEDADA: As usual. Someday you will. I'm late. (*She disappears.*)

PEDRO: Good, now maybe we can get something to drink from him. Oh yi! Heh, you, junkie!

MOROSE: (*smiling*) I beg your pardon.

PEDRO: It's all right. You're a junkie, I'm a drunk. Same difference. I'm an easy fellow to get along with.

RAFAEL: I easier than he.

MOROSE: I like you. (*Gives bottle to Pedro.*) I need a chorus. Do you all want to be my chorus?

PEDRO: (*turning toward Gongora*) Heh, Gon. He needs a chorus.

GONGORA: May I speak a threni?

PEDRO: You and your goddamn threnis. You old fool.

MOROSE: (*looking at Pedro, and then at the others*) Okay?

CHORUS: Okay.

[*Darkness.*]

Scene 3

The Chorus and the Prayer

MOROSE: All right, shall we all bow our heads for a few moments in prayer?

> *[Pedro and Rafael look at each other in amazement. They pause a moment, then bow their heads in prayer, rather uncomfortably.]*

Let us say a prayer for the whole state of Christ Church. (*Long pause.*) My prayer should be (*reflects*) that men everywhere should have bread and peace (*pause*), assuming of course that they want bread and peace. Or may they have bread and circuses if that is more to their liking.

GONGORA: *Panem et circensis* is the way of men.

MOROSE: All right, that's enough. Don't we all feel a little better now?

> *[The three wag their heads obediently.]*

(*Pause.*) You know, to be young, gifted, and black is to be fucked up.

> *[The Chorus stares at him.]*

Very, very fucked up.

GONGORA: It is a malady of the age.

MOROSE: Yeah, malady of the age. Everywhere that I have ever been in my life, I have seen men suffer. Suffer to such a degree that it often caused me to wonder at the variety of ways that a man may suffer between his birth and his death.

GONGORA: Don't speak about that. It's unpleasant.

MOROSE: All right. May I say that I have suffered the hells of this world.

GONGORA: And why you as opposed to another?

MOROSE: Because I more than any other know the implications of my history.

GONGORA: The implications of your history?

MOROSE: I more than any other know what it all means.

GONGORA: Tell them of the nice things, they want to hear of the nice things. Just like in the movies.

MOROSE: (*to audience*) All right. There are those who hold up the tent of my life. There is Soledada, whom you have already met, and Celestina who is the night. Soledada doesn't really hate my addiction. It's just that whenever she opens her mouth her mother's voice comes out. I love her very much though, because she's a very good person, so very different from myself. I like also walking a great deal. Like this. (*Walks around stage.*) It gives me the illusion that I'm free or something.

GONGORA: I've traveled many hells, lived in the underworld both as a man and a woman.

MOROSE: Both as a man and a woman, damn, suffered twice, eh?

GONGORA: Yes, it was a certain curse that they put on me because I saw too much. I think it was because I saw my father naked. But it was so long ago I can't remember anymore.

MOROSE: Well, having lived both as a woman and a man, is there anything of the world that you can tell me?

GONGORA: (*Long pause.*) Life sometimes is not kind.

> *[Pedro runs up to him and kicks the cane from beneath him.]*

> *[Darkness.]*

Scene 4

Night Scene and "Alba"

Night Scene

> *[Soledada returns home. She bears several packages in her arms. Morose is seated at the table which he uses for a desk. Chorus is watching from stage right.]*

MOROSE: Sweetheart.

> *[Soledada places packages on the floor.]*

SOLEDADA: Hi.

MOROSE: Yes, very.

SOLEDADA: Yes, very what?

MOROSE: (*seeing that she totally misses the pun*) You said hi, and I said yes, I am very *high*, get it?

SOLEDADA: Getting weirder every day.

MOROSE: That too. (*Morose takes money from her pocketbook while her back is turned.*)

[*Soledada walks wearily to put away her coat and bags somewhere offstage.*]

Soledada, why is it that it takes up to three hours for you to thaw out after you get home?

SOLEDADA: I'm sorry. You know how I am. I'm moody, I guess. It must be my sign.

MOROSE: (*embracing her*) Everything is going to work out just fine. Better days ahead.

SOLEDADA: Why is everything going to work out? It never has before.

MOROSE: Somehow I can't help but feel that the angel of mercy is secretly looking over my life.

SOLEDADA: Oh, shit, are we back to the angel of mercy again? (*She pushes him away.*)

MOROSE: (*going back to his diagram on the desk*) No, really, I think there's a change coming.

SOLEDADA: Why, are you going get a job?

MOROSE: (*long stare*) I didn't say something cataclysmic, I just said something good is going to happen.

SOLEDADA: I don't ask much of you, do I? I mean, I'm not one of those castrating black women that you're always talking about, am I? (*She waits for answer; he looks at her.*) Well?

MOROSE: No, dear, you're not one of those castrating black women that I'm always speaking about.

SOLEDADA: I'm serious.

MOROSE: All right then, seriously. No, you're not very demanding. You're very sweet and you're very beautiful. And you're as understanding as one can be (*pause*) who comes from a fucked-up, middle-class, Negro-New England family.

SOLEDADA: Well?

MOROSE: Right, given the circumstances you're very nice.

SOLEDADA: You're so bright, aren't you? Got something smart to say every time your mouth jumps open. Always got an answer for everything. You so busy being Morose. You can't hear me. Got to have a full-time pity. You're only crying for one person and that's always Morose. If you're so bright then why don't you save yourself, you know.

MOROSE: Honey, I can't get a job if that's what you mean.

SOLEDADA: Just for a little . . .

[82]

MOROSE: No. I'm at the point that contact with those people will lead to murder. I swear. I'm not joking.

SOLEDADA: Just a part-time . . .

MOROSE: No way! I'll try to sell some of the children's stories I wrote for you. I'll do anything . . . else than work.

SOLEDADA: Oh, nigger.

[She walks away angrily. Morose walks over to Pedro who is witnessing the scene from stage right.]

MOROSE: What is it you want of me, world?

PEDRO: We want you to labor, Nigger.

MOROSE: Labor at what?

PEDRO: It doesn't matter just as long as you don't enjoy it.

MOROSE: But what about my art?

PEDRO: You're black, aren't you?

MOROSE: Yes.

PEDRO: Black people aren't allowed art.

MOROSE: (as if he were a child that had just been rebuked) Oh, damn, I forgot.

Alba

[Pedro ushers the other two of the Chorus about the stage. He commands them to be still.]

PEDRO: Shh, come on there, silence. Morose is reciting his "Alba." It's one of the few good moments.

MOROSE: (*walks reverentially to center stage*)

"Alba."

Esta la noche del silencio.
The city is a girl with new breasts.
She sheds screams
the way an old woman sheds odors.
My alba is:
La noche del silencio.
The city is a girl with new breasts.

[Darkness.]

Scene 5

MOROSE: (*handing cellophane bag to Pedro*) Here you go, man. Be careful, this shit is pure.

PEDRO: Yeah, okay. (*Takes out syringe.*)

MOROSE: I didn't know this was your thing, too.

[84]

PEDRO: It's not. This is for the blind one. He's like you.

MOROSE: Like me?

PEDRO: He talks a lot of shit, but he's a junkie, too.

MOROSE: Damn, a blind junkie.

PEDRO: Okay, blindie, take off your jacket. (*Looking at jacket.*) Damn, this is a raggedy motherfucker here. All right, give me your arm (*injects needle*).

RAFAEL: (*looks on in disgust*) You people crazy, man.

MOROSE: Damn, Pedro, why you so cruel?

PEDRO: Got to be cruel, baby; otherwise people run the fuck all over you.

RAFAEL: It's when he was in jail.

PEDRO: No, that ain't it. I was always this way and it don't have shit to do with my sign or anything like that.

MOROSE: Why did they put you in jail?

PEDRO: 'Cause I raped some jive bitch. Is that cool?

MOROSE: All right with me, man. Why'd you rape her?

PEDRO: She really wanted me to rape her anyway. One of the silly country bitches, talking that stiff shit like: "I don't know if I should." That's because I was too dark for her. But I had a surprise for her ass.

MOROSE: So you went to jail.

PEDRO: For three years, but I got off. I kept writing her in prison and made her get me off because she felt guilty.

MOROSE: You must be a pretty good writer.

PEDRO: Listen, man, all bitches are come freaks.

MOROSE: Oh yeah!

PEDRO: They all want you to rape them. Just like they want you to hurt them.

RAFAEL: (*laughing*) Pedro the pimp.

PEDRO: You're damn right. In one year I had that same bitch out on the street hustling for me.

RAFAEL: Ha-ha, a *chulo*.

PEDRO: No, baby, *chulisimo*. A master-pimp. (*Looks at Morose.*) You're like the blind one, all that knowledge and poor as a motherfucker. If I had what you had I'd be a millionaire by now. You two just don't have no heart.

GONGORA: Pedro . . . tell me . . .

PEDRO: Tell you what?

GONGORA: What am I wearing?

PEDRO: You're wearing a tuxedo, a blue tuxedo.

MOROSE: Why you going to lie to him?

PEDRO: Shut up, I'm having some fun.

[86]

GONGORA: Am I clean?

PEDRO: Very clean. Your shirt is silk and your boots are well polished.

GONGORA: No one must see me dirty.

PEDRO: None will, old man.

GONGORA: Why are the wheels turning so quickly?

PEDRO: Because of the wind, old man.

GONGORA: They laughed at me and destroyed all my poems.

PEDRO: Who laughed at you?

GONGORA: The people in the town. Then they took my house and land, my woman, my name.

RAFAEL: When people rob you they take everything.

GONGORA: They made me drink until my eyes ran.

PEDRO: All right. I don't want to hear any more.

RAFAEL: Every time he gets high he goes over the same thing.

MOROSE: What people is he talking about?

PEDRO: Who knows? I don't even think he does. Keeps talking some shit about poems being taken from him.

GONGORA: The darkness coming in one wave.

RAFAEL: (*more to himself*) I hate the dark.

PEDRO: Darkness. That ain't no big thing. They did that shit to me, too. You know.

MOROSE: Who did?

PEDRO: When I was in the joint they put me in solitary, you know, in this motherfucking pitch-black hole. Because I got an attitude when some psychiatrist wanted to study me.

MOROSE: A psychiatrist?

PEDRO: Yeah, you know how white people love to study you. This zombie was from Germany. He want to know why I walk like that. Do you ever smile? How did you rape that girl? I told him: "With my motherfucking dick, that's how I did it, you chump!" He tried to make me feel like I wasn't nothing, but I let him know he was definitely no big thing to me. It's just a matter of who's in power at the time.

MOROSE: And they put you in solitary for that?

PEDRO: Yes, and it was black as the inside of a whore's pussy.

RAFAEL: That's white people, man. They are the same the world over.

GONGORA: (*getting to his feet*) I'm Gongora the poet. You know me. I . . . am Gongora the poet. Men have called me genius.

PEDRO: Haul ass, genius.

GONGORA: Pedro, what am I wearing?

PEDRO: You're wearing nothing, old man, you're naked like a fucking dog. Naked, naked, like scum, old man, and God ain't never heard of you.

GONGORA: My suit?

PEDRO: Oh, shit! You such a sorry motherfucker. Your arm is bleeding . . . come here, old man.

GONGORA: (*embarrassed*) Pedro, Pedro.

PEDRO: What, fool?

GONGORA: I have to go to the toilet.

PEDRO: What do you have to do?

GONGORA: Number one, I think.

PEDRO: You have to wash your arm, too. (*Leads him offstage.*)

[*Darkness.*]

Scene 6

[*Morose as the scene opens is found nodding. Rafael is the only other person on stage. He is in a crouched position, elbows resting on thighs. He is observing Morose, who slowly evolves out of his nod.*]

MOROSE: Damn, where am I? Whew, got out there for a second.

RAFAEL: You are on the Lower East Side, in the place they call America, and the Jew is breathing outside at your door.

MOROSE: Thank you, that's right, that's where I am.

RAFAEL: What were you seeing?

MOROSE: I was seeing this girl's ass. (*Pause.*) Think it was Celestina. I don't know for certain. She was moving through a street, morning, I think. And her ass was moving through a street filled with white people and they all had death on their faces. Damn, man, she was moving so *free*, whenever the people looked on her it just reminded them how near to dying they were so that they grew even older when they saw her. She was looking good . . . very good, very good.

RAFAEL: That's what you were seeing.

MOROSE: Went into a nod behind it.

RAFAEL: I don't dream very much. Sometimes I dream but not often. (*Starts to sing in very low voice.*)

> *Eh, eh Bomba heu heu*
> *Conga bafio te*
> *Conga mourne de le*
> *Conga do ki la*
> *Conga li*

But in truth though, they does work niggers here, you know, a blackie have it hard here. (*Thinks a second.*) But blackie does have it hard everywhere. It's the same

[90]

thing home. Dominica, St. Lucia, Aruba is all the same. You does have Dutch master or an English or a Yankee, he master just the same.

MOROSE: Same shit.

RAFAEL: If you cut up he sugar cane, make he rum or he ginger beer or rubber, or serve him he food when he belly groan, if you do that then he love you.

MOROSE: And what do they give you for that?

RAFAEL: Oh they does give you the sky and the rain sometime, and if you really nice, double nice, they may even let you have part of your beach. They's a bitch, man.

MOROSE: Which earth were you from?

RAFAEL: I from the mountains, man, they does call us Rastafari.

MOROSE: Rastafari. (*He likes the word.*)

RAFAEL: My mother use to tell me of a way making a child have lockjaw so he couldn't eat. Cut him along the side of he jawbone, here (*touches Morose*).

MOROSE: Damn!

RAFAEL: So he don't grow up kissing the white man in he ass. But there's a lot of mulatto anyway. And they come to power with those people of the city. They faces does be tight like they master's and they women full of dead.

MOROSE: But where did the mulatto come from?

RAFAEL: The master take him a walk one day. He drink and fart, and he look up so; and he see this black-ass woman, and he decide he want she. Come here, woman, and lift up you damn dress.

MOROSE: And shows her the house.

RAFAEL: And it's far the hell out of the way of the sun. Cloth, nice on she ass. By the time morning come, you have a mulatto.

MOROSE: And who is she who is the mother?

RAFAEL: Any woman who is hungry.

MOROSE: And you?

RAFAEL: Me? I is any man who does walk a dark field. Walking on me shadow. And goat walks like me.

MOROSE: And you wait.

RAFAEL: I don't believe but only half believe this place the hands bring me to.

MOROSE: Not waiting for the resurrection of the flesh?

RAFAEL: Watching from behind my eyes as they step over me, like as if I a dog scratching he ass in the road. They step over me.

MOROSE: And you wait.

RAFAEL: And I wait, Lord, you know, because murder is a luxury, and I can't afford it yet, not yet. And so I wait, and the Kasta waits.

Eh, eh Bomba heu heu
Conga bafio te
Conga mourne de le
Conga do ki la
Conga li

[Darkness.]

Scene 7

The Coming of the Father

*[Morose and Soledada at home. He is studying some
sketches on the table and occasionally snorts heroin.
Chorus is stage left.]*

GONGORA: Night. The hour of the suicides. A man is
coming.

RAFAEL: He does not want to come. He will go away.

GONGORA: No, he must come.

[The sound of knocking is heard.]

SOLEDADA: There's somebody at the door.

MOROSE: No, it's probably the sound of the rats dying
between the walls.

[Knocking heard again.]

SOLEDADA: No, someone's there.

MOROSE: It will go away.

GONGORA: Not this time, Morose.

[*Soledada goes to door and peeps through.*]

SOLEDADA: There's a man at the door. He's got on a white suit.

MOROSE: Here. (*He gives her bags of dope.*)

[*Soledada hides dope inside her pants, clears off table, and goes to door.*]

SOLEDADA: (*returning with man dressed in white suit. He seems very affected in his manner. He is in late forties.*) This man says he wants to see you.

EL CID: I thought you'd look more like me. Are you Morose?

MOROSE: Usually.

EL CID: I've had reports on you. They said you were an artist.

MOROSE: I'm sorry.

EL CID: What is this here? (*Looking at plans of a building.*)

MOROSE: I was working on Parnassus.

EL CID: An architect! I'm your father or you're my son, whichever way you prefer. I left your mother in Trinidad. I guess I left you, too.

MOROSE: Oh, OK.

EL CID: It wasn't all quite that simple, although in a way it was. What did she ever say about me?

MOROSE: She said you went off to become a priest in a leper colony.

EL CID: And you believed that.

MOROSE: Well . . . yes.

EL CID: You're really rather naive, aren't you? Well, that's good, I guess. I'm not very naive or very trusting.

MOROSE: Why have you decided to show now?

EL CID: Because I'm not happy.

MOROSE: Oh. He's not happy (*to Soledada*).

EL CID: I have some money for you which you'll want, I suppose.

MOROSE: *Deus ex machina.*

EL CID: No, my name is Cid.

MOROSE: No, I meant—never mind. Yes, I could use money.

EL CID: Walk out with me. I don't trust this neighborhood alone.

MOROSE: (*turning to audience*) Street scene.

EL CID: (*with top hat on and hands behind his back,*

casually) So what kind of a person are you? Are you good?

MOROSE: No, I'm not a very good person.

EL CID: Your mother was a good person.

MOROSE: Yes, she was.

EL CID: I should have married her, I might have been much better off.

MOROSE: Perhaps.

[Darkness.]

Scene 8

Rafael Speaks

[Gongora, Pedro, and Rafael have just witnessed the preceding scene.]

RAFAEL: How good it is to be loved by God.

PEDRO: How the fuck would you know, you derelict?

RAFAEL: I don't, but I does know what it feels like to want his love and not get it.

[Pedro stares at him.]

[Darkness.]

Scene 9

Monk's "Misterioso."

MOROSE:
Why I take dope, a soliloquy.
I take dope because my eyes hurt.
The women's faces put pain on me
in the city, which is a swamp.
And they call it New York or Philadelphia
or Washington or Boston but my eyes still hurt
and so I take dope
to see without the pain of seeing.
And the vivid houses plot against me
crossways along the dark.
And art makes me over
and I take
dope.

[Darkness.]

Scene 10

The Dice Game and Celestina

[Downstage Pedro and Rafael are hotly engaged in a dice game. Gongora is seated upon his cane chair. Upstage Morose is embracing Celestina, a very dark-skinned black woman. He gets on his knees and starts to bite her thighs and buttocks while she continually pushes him away (lightly). We cannot hear their conversation, thus their actions are mimetic behind the argument of Pedro and Rafael.]

PEDRO: (*shaking dice passionately*) Puta, madre, puta, madre, coño! (*He shoots dice.*) Dammit, these dice run away from me like a woman.

RAFAEL: I don't blame them, the way you smell. (*Laughs.*)

PEDRO: (*suddenly pulling out knife*) How do I smell, bato?

RAFAEL: (*very frightened*) Smell? Oh, you don't smell at all.

PEDRO: Are you saying I have no smell, like a virgin?

RAFAEL: Oh, no, no.

PEDRO: Then how is it that I smell?

RAFAEL: Oh, beautiful, like the air in the mountains.

[Pedro puts knife away.]

RAFAEL: (*taking out his knife after he is released*) Don't do that, Pedro. Make joke with you mouth, but if you pull a blade on me again, I'm going kill you. You blackie like me and I does love you, but don't play so.

PEDRO: (*stares at him for a long pause*) Yeah, okay, cool. (*He turns to Gongora.*) Gongora, blindie, I'm talking to you.

GONGORA: Yes.

PEDRO: Give me that watch of yours.

GONGORA: This watch was my father's; it is very dear to me.

PEDRO: What have I to do with what's dear to you, old fool? Give it here.

GONGORA: (*pauses for a moment, then withdraws watch from inside of his coat*) Here.

PEDRO: You can't even see to piss straight. What need have you for a watch? Here, Rafael, I'll bet you this watch against all I owe you.

RAFAEL: All right.

[The spotlight falls on Morose and Celestina now.]

CELESTINA: No, you can't have some.

MOROSE: Oh, baby, just let me kiss it a little bit.

CELESTINA: I know you don't want to hear the truth, but I'm going to run it to you anyway. You say that you're tired. Motherfucker, who in the world is more tired than us? How long have we been dying, dying and waiting for you sorry people to get yourselves together?

MOROSE: (*falling to floor in melodramatic motion*) Mercy, sister.

CELESTINA: Mercy, what mercy have you all given us? You got every kind of jones in the world. You got a drug habit, a pussy habit, a self-pity habit, and what it's really all about is that you got a coward habit. That's what you got.

MOROSE: Me coward, me coward.

CELESTINA: You damn sure are. If you so-called black men would have done something when you saw us bein' raped and dragged over here on them slave ships, this whole out-to-lunch shit would have never gone down. But no, you'll always be talking 'bout: "Well, we got to survive." Niggers have never been willing to die, for anything. Except their own addiction. Maybe a few of them died in fights over women, yet it's never really about us. You dig. Now I'm tired of hanging out with dudes who are just going to drag me down. What do you have to offer but those sorry-ass artist changes of yours?

MOROSE: (*softly*) Honey, whatever you need to survive, I hope you get it. I hope you find some rich dude.

CELESTINA: There aren't any young rich men.

MOROSE: Well, I hope you find one that's not too old.

CELESTINA: Me too. Can you let me hold some change for some cigarettes?

MOROSE: Ain't got none.

CELESTINA: See, that's what I mean.

MOROSE: OK, we're very fucked up. We've been so busy trying to define ourselves we haven't even gotten around to you. I know that.

[Celestina turns away from him slowly.]

I'll get in the wind, and leave you alone. But please . . .

CELESTINA: Yes?

MOROSE: Let me get a little piece of pussy once more before I go.

CELESTINA: That's all it's about with you, eh? I almost took you serious.

MOROSE: Listen, I meant everything I said. So what? I still want you. Fucked up as I am or not, I still want you.

CELESTINA: Yeah, well, you go on wanting, sucker. (She goes to walk away from him.)

MOROSE: Rape time, people.

CELESTINA: Listen, you can't go on acting like a baby.

[Morose starts biting her again, starts ripping clothes off her.]

[101]

All right, all right, you're crazy.

[He suddenly stops his attack and bends over like a child.]

MOROSE: Damn, I'm sick, baby. I don't feel good.

CELESTINA: What's the matter?

MOROSE: I feel sick.

CELESTINA: You want something to drink?

MOROSE: No, I got to go (*exits*).

[Darkness.]

Scene 11

Morose and La Pasionaria

[Scene takes place in the park.]

[La Pasionaria walks over to Morose. She is a slender, beautiful Puerto Rican girl who occasionally betrays sadness. Her eyes are beautiful eyes when she is half nodding. Sometimes she forgets her train of thought because of the stupor of drugs.]

LA PASIONARIA: Hey, man, what's happening?

MOROSE: You're late.

LA PASIONARIA: Yeah, yeah, man, wow, really sorry, I got into cleaning my house. Kept seeing bloodspots on the floor. I hate that.

MOROSE: Did you cop?

LA PASIONARIA: What? Oh yeah, here you go, man. (*She gives him cellophane bag.*)

MOROSE: (*opens bag and snorts*) You're a gentle woman.

LA PASIONARIA: Uh hum (*agrees with him*).

MOROSE: Pasionaria, when are you going to give me some pussy?

LA PASIONARIA: (*slightly nodding*) What you say?

MOROSE: I said, when are you going to give me some of your fine Puerto Rican pussy?

LA PASIONARIA: I ain't never going to give it up to you. Anyway, Tito would kill you . . . (*pause*) and me.

MOROSE: It would be worth it.

LA PASIONARIA: To you maybe.

MOROSE: You know, you are my sister. You can tell by that big ass of yours that the white man raped your mama just like he did mine.

LA PASIONARIA: (*looks behind herself at her ass*) Yeah, I know I'm your sister. So what you want to fuck your sister for? That's incest, ain't it?

MOROSE: Well, I dig incest.

LA PASIONARIA: Hey, look man, I'm into a lot of coke these days, so I don't want to go through these scag changes no more. So like, you going to have to get it together somewhere else.

MOROSE: Wow, cocaine, moving upper class these days.

LA PASIONARIA: Well, I got my brother Julio, and I'm trying to get him some money so he can go back to P.R. 'Cause he's walking around all hairy with a beard and everything. Looks like a *jíbaro* or something. Got to get him out of here. This place is killing him. Can't nobody live here.

MOROSE: Tell me, do you scratch a man up when you come?

LA PASIONARIA: Ask Tito if you want to know so bad.

MOROSE: I'm asking you.

LA PASIONARIA: You know, you too fresh. You don't know how to talk to people.

MOROSE: (*gives her four dollars*) I'm a little short.

LA PASIONARIA: You always a little short. Hey, don't call me no more. All right? (*She exits.*)

[*Darkness.*]

Scene 12

Gongora's Soliloquy

[Gongora alone on stage, seated in his cane seat. He pulls out a kerchief from inside pocket, locates his nose, blows it (pause), *then speaks.]*

GONGORA: Quintilian was the first artist to be supported by the state. He taught school in Rome. A pretty good poet, too. They promised me that I could recite a threni later on. They lie to me so much though, I can't put too much faith in what they tell me. (*Pause.*) I don't exactly know what to say about this young man Morose. I don't know whether to put him in heaven or hell. I don't know where he'll put himself. His love for Soledada is *buen amor* but his love of Celestina is definitely *loco amor*. He says that he does not curse God for bringing him into the world too late, for he thinks it would have been harder for him were he born before. Likewise he does not curse God for being born too early, for he knows that the next generation will be more desperate than the world has ever known. He says that he curses God for being born *at all*. He has a good mind, yes, but I don't think he's a very nice person. (*He begins to take up cane to walk away.*) I only thank God that I never had children. It's always the wrong time for them.

[Darkness.]

Scene 13

A Doll's House Revisited

[El Cid leads Morose into the living room of his house. Eric Satie's "Deux pensées devant trois" is heard. He introduces Morose to a young light-skinned girl seated in corner, slender, with amazed but comforting eyes.]

EL CID: Morose, this is Melibea, my niece. She knows more about me than anyone living.

MELIBEA: I don't know quite that much. Hello, is it really Morose?

MOROSE: Yes, it is.

EL CID: Melibea plays the cello, dances, paints and plays chess.

MOROSE: All at the same time?

MELIBEA: No, only one at a time.

EL CID: My son is an architect-writer. I saw a picture of Chartres and Cluny; he likes cathedrals. You didn't inherit art from me or your mother. I wonder where it came from.

MOROSE: I have two questions for you. Melibea, I'm sorry

if I bore you for a while, but I have to find this out.

MELIBEA: Don't mind me.

EL CID: Go ahead and ask.

MOROSE: Firstly, why did you bring me into this world, to sit around and watch leaves die? Secondly, having brought me into this, why did you then decide to leave me?

EL CID: You want me to answer those?

MOROSE: Yes.

EL CID: (*pausing, looking first at Melibea and then at Morose*) The answer to the first is, it was an accident. The answer to the second, it seemed a good idea. The most sensible thing I could do after you were born was to leave you. It's that simple.

MOROSE: (*thoughtfully*) All right.

EL CID: No, it's not all right, but that's just the way it is.

MOROSE: Well, while you were away finding out that you weren't happy, I've been falling into addiction . . . art and a few other things.

EL CID: Why in God's name would you choose art, as bad as things were?

MOROSE: It seemed the most graceful form of suicide.

[Melibea laughs.]

[Darkness.]

Scene 14

Morose Enters His Father's House Again.

[We enter in medias res. Morose seems feverish. He makes a full circuit of the stage to symbolize another visit with chorus.]

EL CID: You're coming to me for money again? Your nose is running and your hands are shaking. Don't ever come to me with your nose running again. When you come, if you come try to look like my son or at least a man. (*Pause.*) You say you need money. Do you want a job?

MOROSE: I already have a job.

EL CID: Which is what?

MOROSE: My job is finding another face inside my face.

EL CID: (*laughs*) Must not pay too well. How long is it going to take you?

MOROSE: Only as long as I live.

EL CID: Well, that's too long, boy.

MOROSE: Look, I need money.

EL CID: How did you use to survive?

MOROSE: A bit here. A bit there.

EL CID: In other words, you always live off others.

MOROSE: Not exactly, no.

EL CID: How long have you been with Soledada?

MOROSE: For about three years.

EL CID: She is a good woman.

MOROSE: Yes.

EL CID: I will tell you what I am going to do for you. I will give you enough money to go on a world tour with your lady.

MOROSE: World tour?

EL CID: She has earned it. I want you to live well for, say, a year. At the end of this time I want you to return here and deal with the problems of the business.

MOROSE: Your business?

EL CID: Yes.

MOROSE: Which is what?

EL CID: Have three. I have a chain of stores and I own a good bit of real estate.

MOROSE: What kind of stores are these?

EL CID: Liquor stores mainly, you know how your people love to drink. (*He calls offstage.*) Melibea. Melibea.

[*Melibea enters.*]

MELIBEA: Yes, Uncle.

EL CID: Did you get that information for me.

MELIBEA: Yes, Uncle, Bucco says that the strikes in the two plants have been unsuccessful.

EL CID: Expected. (*He turns to Morose.*) You see, even Melibea works. Melibea, do you think you can find something for those three to do? (*He points to Chorus.*)

MELIBEA: Perhaps. Have they any skills?

MOROSE: Rafael, the one on the left, is very good with a razor. Pedro knows a lot about power.

PEDRO: You mean we going to have to work?

EL CID: Don't look so upset, if I don't give my son money you'll all starve. How about the old one, is he sick?

MOROSE: That's Gongora. He is blind, he recites poems.

EL CID: What am I going to do with poems?

GONGORA: It might ease your conscience.

PEDRO: Will you watch your damn mouth, old fool?

EL CID: Don't worry about my conscience. (*Strikes Gongora with cane.*)

PEDRO: (*aside, speaking to Melibea*) Hey, listen, Mama, don't I know you from someplace?

MELIBEA: I doubt it.

PEDRO: You didn't grow up in El Barrio, did you?

MELIBEA: Of course not.

PEDRO: Oh, sorry.

MELIBEA: (*to El Cid*) These boys are from the streets. Maybe you could put them in charge of District Seven and District Nine.

EL CID: Perhaps.

MELIBEA: We can try them out there, you know what you've been saying about Marco.

EL CID: Yes, Marco is getting soft. We can try them out for a while.

MELIBEA: Can the blind one recite what we tell him?

PEDRO: He has a good memory.

GONGORA: I don't like dealing with people.

PEDRO: He can be taught.

EL CID: All right, Melibea, take them out and do what you can.

MELIBEA: Okay, come this way. (*To Pedro.*) Tell me, are you very large?

PEDRO: What?

MELIBEA: Are you very large?

PEDRO: Yeah, I'm large.

MELIBEA: I knew you would say yes.

[They exit.]

MOROSE: What is she going to do?

EL CID: Don't worry about it, I am going to make arrangements for you to leave on the weekend. Let me make out this check. (*Writes check.*)

MOROSE: How did you get started in business?

EL CID: My first big money I made from manufacturing toilet paper.

MOROSE: Is that right?

EL CID: Here (*gives check*). It's not important, however. Tell me, how are you with white women?

MOROSE: What do you mean, how am I?

EL CID: How do you feel about them?

MOROSE: I don't like them, you have to give up too much information. Then you have to give up too much life.

EL CID: Why?

MOROSE: Because they're dead and have to feed on life.

[112]

EL CID: Oh, I see.

MOROSE: Why?

EL CID: It was an idea I had; I'll find something else.

MOROSE: This money to travel?

EL CID: I want you to see the world. I want you to see places where the sun comes almost close enough to be touched. I want you to eat well, you're too thin. I want you to taste . . . everything, then I think we will be able to talk. By the way, you haven't moved from that tenement house yet.

MOROSE: No.

EL CID: Wasn't the place I found for you nice enough?

MOROSE: The people look pretty dry, even for white folks.

EL CID: It's up to you. We'll talk when you come back. I think you'll see it a little differently then.

MOROSE: Oh yeah.

[Darkness.]

Scene 15

Soledada and Morose

[*Night.*]

MOROSE: Harlem, a Hundred sixteenth Street, the street of the cows. The junkies dying like cows. Ain't nobody looking, nobody looking. Feet move past laying cows. Feet hurry themselves to catacombs. Harlem, street of the cows.

SOLEDADA: What you doing, you coming to bed?

MOROSE: No, I'm moving too fast. The world's out there screaming.

SOLEDADA: Why don't you slow on down for a minute?

MOROSE: You suppose to be happy; you always wanted me stop using dope. Okay, here I am. Cling!

SOLEDADA: I am happy, at least you're talking.

MOROSE: Damn, was I all that bad? I thought I used to talk.

SOLEDADA: Here you go, "Soledada, fetch me my calmative."

MOROSE: (*falls to the floor with laughter*) Damn, I'm one crazy nigger.

SOLEDADA: But that was all you had to say, except for "Give me some—"

MOROSE: (*laughing and then slowly falling to serious*) Yeah, it's all right here, for a minute. Right now it's all right. Your skin in front of these walls fits right. You walk through all this death so easy. That's good.

SOLEDADA: I don't walk through anything easy.

MOROSE: Randolph told me, but I wasn't going to listen, see.

SOLEDADA: Who is Randolph?

MOROSE: I told you about Randolph.

SOLEDADA: Never told me.

MOROSE: See, Randolph was my teacher. Taught me colors, space. Was a master, like Bird or somebody. 'Cause he said a canvas was a street and, see, people are trapped inside. Love hard enough you free them. One move, child could happen.

SOLEDADA: (*now totally in his dream*) Yeah. That's why I'm with you.

MOROSE: Why?

SOLEDADA: Never mind, keep going.

MOROSE: So my eyes are open now, right. Start noticing walls where sky should be.

SOLEDADA: Architecture?

MOROSE: Yeah, except I'm moving too fast to draw a straight line. But I know this (*shows her the palm of his right hand*), the open hand of God. And me walking dead in the middle, that's what perpendicular means.

SOLEDADA: So what was it Randolph said?

MOROSE: That you carry the history of your race in your body. Black people leave the earth won't be no art. Like the water to the desert. We are. But don't ever expect them to call you artist. Don't ever expect. They'll never give you that much respect. And he said it just as calm, just another fact of life, no big thing. But it took me outside when I really found out what he was saying. That can break your motherfucking heart, you know.

SOLEDADA: I know.

MOROSE: No, you don't know. But that's why I started messing with dope, so that I wouldn't have to start dealing with all that.

SOLEDADA: That's what they wanted you to do.

MOROSE: Had to stop thinking for a while.

SOLEDADA: Stop thinking and you're dead. Don't have to stop, just have to relax.

MOROSE: You show me, show me good, I'll follow.

[Darkness.]

Scene 16

[Morose in spotlight, figure of Gongora in background.]

MOROSE: I don't like being alone these days. I get frightened even when she just goes out to shop. Must be because I stopped taking dope. But damn, I didn't know it had that much effect on me. When I leave for this journey around the world I want to be clean. I want to be totally free. I don't want to travel with the disease of my country. You step on a plane and a few hours later you walk out onto different earth. They tell me that anything is possible now. In one day my future is completely different! I guess you can even change water to wine. I've got to learn . . . I've got to learn how to breathe easier. I've got to learn how to talk the talk of people. I've got to learn how to be interested. Maybe Soledada . . . maybe she can teach me. She knows how to be human. Women do it better. She says that I never spoke to her. I love her but . . . you've been asleep, man. Dope puts you to sleep. Gongora!

GONGORA: Yes?

MOROSE: Dope puts you to sleep.

GONGORA: Yes, a beautiful quiet sleep.

MOROSE: But it is the sleep of a dead man, isn't it?

GONGORA: Yes, but so soft.

MOROSE: I went out yesterday without armor, into the streets.

GONGORA: How did it seem without dope?

MOROSE: The city was just a noise of lights.

GONGORA: Yes.

MOROSE: And the people were all dying in their clothes.

GONGORA: Yes.

MOROSE: And I never knew the buildings screamed so loud. It was morning, the time I'm usually just going to bed. You know how sometimes the sun comes on you without warning and all at once you find the night is over.

GONGORA: Yes, I know. (*Pause.*) I remember that much.

MOROSE: The tenement buildings all leaking out workers. Each carrying the smell of his house. And they're still sleepy with the night so they've not yet thought how sad they were today. And the whores along Fourteenth Street, is the look on their faces amazement or terror that the night is over?

GONGORA: (*very excited*) I don't know that. Tell me, colors, colors?

MOROSE: Mostly gray on gray, sometimes green but not earth green, cancer green.

GONGORA: And you were frightened.

MOROSE: Yes, very frightened. It's been a long time since I let myself see that much.

GONGORA: And what were the Jews doing?

MOROSE: They were opening up their markets and gates. They will flee as soon as the dark comes on and the niggers become hungry.

GONGORA: Hungry enough to steal.

MOROSE: Hungry enough to kill and then steal.

[Darkness.]

Scene 17

[The Chorus. Morose has left.]

PEDRO: So you think he is going to stay away from scag?

GONGORA: He wants to live too much to turn around.

RAFAEL: He has a chance if he stays away from this place.

PEDRO: A trip around the world can't last forever. What did you tell him?

GONGORA: I told him to stay away from all cities, to stay close to mountains whenever possible.

RAFAEL: I have told him the same thing.

GONGORA: He loves the two women (*he thinks for a moment*); his love for Soledada is *buen amor* but his love for Celestina must be *loco amor*.

PEDRO: How the fuck do you know what is *buen amor* and what is *loco amor*?

GONGORA: It seems to me that . . .

PEDRO: What do you know about it, how long has it been since you've seen your dick?

GONGORA: I remember.

PEDRO: You remember. If I could kidnap one of them, I would take the dark one. Celestina.

GONGORA: Her body is like the night.

PEDRO: Yes, like night. Soledada is good, you can depend on her, but she is too stiff for me.

RAFAEL: Celestina too moody, wild birds flying over water. Those women leave lines on you face. I know. I take Soledada.

> [*Gongora grows weary of the discussion. He walks away from the two others and leans on cane.*]

PEDRO: Where are you going, old man?

GONGORA: I'm thinking.

PEDRO: You and Morose, that's all you two do is think. He at least has a rich father. That's the only thing that saved him, otherwise he would still be thinking and strung out like a dog.

GONGORA: You're angry because we at least have our art. That's why you hate us.

PEDRO: Art, what the fuck is art?

GONGORA: You have nothing, no music, no words, no thought, nothing but yourself and you can't stand it that anyone else has more.

PEDRO: What does that make you? A saint because you have art? If I was not your eyes where would you be? Artist, ain't that a bitch. When you were hungry you damn sure wasn't talking about art then. I was the one who stole so we could eat. If it wasn't for me and Rafael you would be dead, you old faggot. But you always have to act superior. You act like everyone else is just your servant.

GONGORA: It frightens you that there's something you can't understand.

PEDRO: Understand. Shit, there's nothing I can't understand that's real. I understand that this is a world full of white people that have money and power. I understand that the only way they'll let you live is if you sing for them, fuck them, clean up after them or cook for them.

RAFAEL: That's true enough.

PEDRO: That's real, I can understand that. I can understand that if you don't have food you die; if you don't have money, nobody but your mother will want to see you and she damn well might not. You are the one that's ignorant, you are the one that can't understand. But the next time you run that "I am an artist" bullshit to me,

I'm going to cut your ass (*pulls out knife*). Then maybe you will learn who is afraid.

GONGORA: You're a child.

PEDRO: Oh yeah, I'm a child. (*He runs over and knocks Gongora to the ground.*)

RAFAEL: Come on, Pedro. You don't have to do that.

PEDRO: He has to learn what is real.

GONGORA: (*trying to get up*) You think because you have strength that you have the only understanding.

PEDRO: Stay down, dog, otherwise I'll knock you down again. (*He places his foot on Gongora's chest.*) Here now, I'm standing on your chest. Write me a poem to make me get off.

RAFAEL: Pedro!

PEDRO: No, I want to teach this wise man. Go on, artist, use words tender enough to move my heart. Make me moral, poet. Do you think you can? Can you make me feel guilty? And if I had raped your woman or your mother or had put chains on you, what could you create that would move me enough to repent?

GONGORA: Nothing.

PEDRO: Louder.

GONGORA: Nothing, I have no words.

PEDRO: You're damn right you don't (*lifts foot*). So much for art. (*He exits laughing.*)

[122]

RAFAEL: You a fool for arguing with him.

GONGORA: It was because I said something that frightened him. I should be more careful not to frighten people. They don't like to be intimidated.

RAFAEL: You frightened him?

GONGORA: What is the time now?

RAFAEL: It is evening, six o'clock.

GONGORA: The workers are returning to their caves. Are they less frightened?

RAFAEL: (*looking out into audience*) They seem less frightened than at morning.

[*Darkness.*]

Scene 18

South Africa

[*Nightclub in black district. Morose and Soledada are dancing amid several other couples. The atmosphere is one of poverty, the smell of sweat and Johannesburg. The stage is lit green and blue. The movement is ecstasy.*]

[*Darkness.*]

Scene 19

Campos Verdaderos

> *[Morose and Soledada are aboard ship off Europe. The time is one year later. He seems much healthier outwardly. She clutches his arm, and they look out over audience. Surreal fantasy of the middle class.]*

SOLEDADA: Wave over there, the ocean's screaming.

MOROSE: Hmm.

SOLEDADA: I'm glad you decided to stop taking planes. You can't see anything from a plane.

MOROSE: Yes, you can.

SOLEDADA: But it's not as beautiful as this.

MOROSE: See that lump of wave over there?

SOLEDADA: Where?

MOROSE: Wait a second, it will come back . . . there.

SOLEDADA: Oh yes.

MOROSE: It looks like you in bed. You know the way you curl up.

SOLEDADA: You're the one that curls up into a little ball.

MOROSE: Well, anyway, your ass always sticks up like a new island.

SOLEDADA: You like it though, don't you?

MOROSE: Um hmm.

SOLEDADA: Well, then. (*Pause.*) I'm so happy, I don't think I was ever so happy in my life. I loved Paris.

MOROSE: (*sings*) I love Paris . . .

SOLEDADA: You know . . . I thought Africa would have been much different.

MOROSE: What you expect, Tarzan or something?

SOLEDADA: Different from what it was. Most of those people acted just the way my parents do. You could easily have passed for a prince or something.

MOROSE: A prince.

SOLEDADA: Now that we have some money.

MOROSE: No, not now that we have some money. I was always a prince, a landless prince.

SOLEDADA: But you have to admit it's easier now, don't you?

MOROSE: No, not easier, just more vast. Everywhere I go in the world, the only thing I see is white people having fun at somebody else's expense. Why is that?

SOLEDADA: Well, we may as well go home then, if that's the way you really feel.

MOROSE: Yes, that's the way I really feel. (*Pause.*) You know how my father made his fortunes?

SOLEDADA: In big business, wasn't it?

MOROSE: By taking over a toilet-paper concern.

SOLEDADA: Really? Well, what difference, what if he were an undertaker? Business, isn't it? What I mean is that it really doesn't have anything to do with you.

MOROSE: Makes me the heir to a toilet-paper concern.

SOLEDADA: Let's not think about it. Let's just dream a little while longer, please. I don't want to wake up yet. Not yet.

MOROSE: Sweet thing. (*He pauses again.*) Where did I find you?

SOLEDADA: Where?

MOROSE: You were sliding along the corridors of colonialism and I snatched you.

SOLEDADA: (*laughing*) Why?

MOROSE: Because you were the better part of the dream, the better part.

[*Darkness.*]

Scene 20

Melibea's Soliloquy

MELIBEA: Yes, I understand my uncle. I understand him very well. He likes to see me dressed up and walking out into the day. So I dress for him. He likes to see me happy so I try to stay happy for him. It's not that hard to do, really.

He likes to play businessman, man, likes power, the weight of power. All right, so I play secretary for him. His little mulatto niece.

How do I feel about black men? It's hard to say. I guess basically I don't believe in them. They just can't quite get it together. True, they have a lot against them, I can see that, but they're just doomed, I guess. I mean, they might make it but it won't be in my lifetime and I can't wait until the next life, you know.

Look at Morose for example. He's going to try and take on America armed with a T square and a ruler, right? and a habit. That's really precious, but come on, doesn't he see what it's all about?

I don't know why my uncle is wasting all this money on him. Maybe he feels guilty about making so much money off dope when he found out his own son was a junkie.

So let Morose have his world tour, let him get cleansed, he'll be back to work on the plantation with the rest of us.

Yes, I understand my uncle; I understand him very well.

Scene 21

The Return

[Soledada and Morose have just returned from their world travels. The scene opens with Morose very seriously involved in kissing Soledada. He kisses her three times and three different ways. He is studying her.]

SOLEDADA: The lights of the city looked like ribbons, didn't they?

MOROSE: From the plane?

SOLEDADA: Yeah, they didn't look real. And did you notice how strange the hallways looked where we came up?

MOROSE: Everything looks tighter, smaller maybe.

SOLEDADA: More frightening. It's going to take me about three months to get used to this place again. Everybody is running so fast.

[The Chorus enters.]

Your friends.

MOROSE: Gongora, Rafael, Pedro, how are you?

GONGORA: Well. You came home finally.

PEDRO: You must really be crazy. I didn't think you would come back.

RAFAEL:

> Goat does come back
> Bird does come back
> Dog does come back

[Soledada is uncomfortable in their presence. She busies herself putting things away.]

PEDRO: What did you bring us?

MOROSE: (*laughing*) How do you know I brought you anything?

RAFAEL: He forget us, man.

GONGORA: He couldn't forget us.

MOROSE: (*opening a valise*) No, I didn't forget you. Have you all been working for my father?

GONGORA: Your father is a peculiar man.

PEDRO: Your father is a motherfucker, is what he is. You know, he wanted us to hustle for him. He's got so many rackets going it's a wonder he don't get dizzy.

MOROSE: That's what I thought. Here, Pedro, I brought you some guava berry wine.

PEDRO: Yeah, for me, that's beautiful, man.

MOROSE: It's for all of you.

PEDRO: All right, all right, I'll share it. Don't panic, people.

MOROSE: And some *cassaver* bread. (*He divides up the thin, dry crackerlike bread.*) I'll get some cups for the wine.

PEDRO: No, that's okay, we can drink it from the bottle. You know, man, that cousin of yours, Melibea, is a witch.

MOROSE: I figured.

PEDRO: She tried to make a stud out of me, which is cool, but she don't even want to leave you your balls. (*He drinks wine and passes it.*)

RAFAEL: (*drinking*) He a bitch, man, I never work for him again.

PEDRO: We were supposed to be his henchmen. He damn near got us killed, too.

MOROSE: Rafael, I brought this knife for you. I got it in West Africa. (*He passes knife to Rafael.*)

RAFAEL: It's beautiful; I can feel the weight of it. This was made by one man. You can feel the care.

MOROSE: Gongora, I brought you the bell; it's from India.

PEDRO: Damn, it looks like gold. (*He gives it to Gongora, who shakes it.*)

GONGORA: It has a beautiful sound.

MOROSE: And for you, Pedro, I brought this whip.

PEDRO: Hot damn, just what I need. It's good leather. (*He starts to crack whip.*)

GONGORA: Did you see anything in Europe?

MOROSE: A lot of death there, a lot of tombs.

GONGORA: You should have expected that.

MOROSE: White people keep trying to figure out how to force a triangle into a circle. Their art is only a geometric game.

GONGORA: What did you think they were going to do, take on the universe, or deal with themselves or something?

MOROSE: Architecture is supposed to be for breathing. It's supposed to make you want to breathe right.

GONGORA: You know, I haven't been drinking since you left. Staying away from the dope, too.

MOROSE: Oh no, that's beautiful, man. Shit, go on! I knew you could. I been feeling pretty good myself. You know, got free for a minute.

GONGORA: The sun's been much . . . (*thinks for a minute*) warmer.

MOROSE: Oh, man, you should have seen it in Africa. Divided the world in two parts.

GONGORA: I was someplace the earth bent over me warm and close, but I found I was asleep.

MOROSE: I'll tell you what's paradise, man.

GONGORA: How do you see it?

MOROSE: I see paradise as not having to kill your own body every day.

PEDRO: Well, are you ready now to become your father's son?

RAFAEL: (*in mockery*) It's time for true.

MOROSE: I don't think I make that.

PEDRO: You finally got the world by the balls. You're not going to let it pass, are you?

GONGORA: You are to assume your father's house.

MOROSE: It's such a boring house.

PEDRO: You don't know that. You got any idea how much money that joker's got?

MOROSE: They never let you have anything for nothing. I've seen that much.

RAFAEL: You've been living well these last few months, you've done a lot of traveling; do you really think you can live in this place anymore?

PEDRO: He's talking shit, Morose ain't about to give that money up.

MOROSE: What would you do?

PEDRO: You know damn well what I'd do. He's your pops, ain't he? He owes you.

MOROSE: He waited all those years, now he comes out of the night with his basket of goodies.

PEDRO: Right, so take the basket.

MOROSE: But I don't like him.

PEDRO: You don't have to like him to take his money.

MOROSE: But his money has such a history.

PEDRO: Fuck history, you keep thinking about that, you'll end up in the nut house.

MOROSE: What do you think, Gongora?

GONGORA: I don't like him either. He kills people without looking.

MOROSE: Rafael?

RAFAEL: He a white man, he always be a white man.

PEDRO: He's got that big-ass house.

GONGORA: In this world you need help.

MOROSE: And how about you, Gongora, you have so much anger and you keep it with you.

GONGORA: Where should I put it?

MOROSE: Not in your arm, that's for sure.

GONGORA: I'm . . . blind; perhaps that's why I can forgive more.

[133]

MOROSE: Maybe, but I doubt it. The only thing I know for certain is that I don't want to ever look like my father.

GONGORA: There is no way to avoid that.

MOROSE: Yes, there is.

[They all look at him.]

RAFAEL: The son does build the house but is the father who own the stone.

[Darkness.]

Scene 22

Celestina and Morose

CELESTINA: Where have you been? I was hoping you were dead or . . . something. You supposed to have been so sick.

MOROSE: Still alive.

CELESTINA: What shit you running today?

MOROSE: Nothing. I just came to bring you something.

CELESTINA: What you bring me?

MOROSE: The only thing that a black woman can believe.

CELESTINA: Must be some money then.

MOROSE: Right.

CELESTINA: You got some money (*in absolute shock*).

[*Morose takes out a thousand dollars in ten-dollar bills and spreads them all around Celestina.*]

Well, fuck a duck.

MOROSE: That's for you, honey. I hope it brings you some happiness for a minute.

CELESTINA: How much is it?

MOROSE: A thousand dollars. People kill their fathers for that much. (*He turns to go.*)

CELESTINA: Wait a minute, don't you want anything?

MOROSE: Do you think that all I think about is pussy?

CELESTINA: When you weren't thinking about dope that's all I ever knew you to think about. By the way, where did you get this money from?

MOROSE: Why?

CELESTINA: Did you steal it?

MOROSE: Why?

CELESTINA: 'Cause I don't want to go to nobody's jail, that's why.

MOROSE: You wouldn't be going. I'd be the one going to jail.

CELESTINA: That's true. Why you giving me this money?

MOROSE: I don't want you to get old and mess up my dream. (*He turns again to go.*)

CELESTINA: Mess up *your* dream. You think I want to get old? A thousand dollars can't stop that.

MOROSE: Catch you later.

CELESTINA: Where you going?

MOROSE: Home.

CELESTINA: No, you not.

MOROSE: I'm not?

CELESTINA: No.

[*Darkness.*]

Scene 23

Soledada's Soliliquy

SOLEDADA: (*waking from nightmare into nightmare*) Morose, Mo-rose? Oh . . . gone. Damn, it's so hot. (*Looking around room.*) They make these houses to die in. I shouldn't have smoked that roach he left on the table. Am I still high? Shut up now. Every time you get scared you start running your damn mouth. Act like you enjoy being frightened. I'm just tired, that's all. Tired of looking between bars. Other windows have bars with faces between them looking. Damn, is it that smoke that's got me? I got to stop doing this to myself. What was it I was just thinking about? Lord, if I'm high let it hurry up and wear off. Why can't I stop being afraid of what's in back of me? Keep seeing all these faces. Stop being hard on yourself. You were just dreaming. Something running and close behind me. Something always behind me. But then I went back to school in my dream. That's because I was free there for a minute. Didn't have to deal with people, just books. Only nigger there? No, that fat girl Helena was there, always dressed like she was from New York. I could tell the first time I saw her she'd never stayed in New York for any length of time. She didn't look tired and drained like New York women. Yes, Helena Jordan. Only two. Class full of white girls, perfume, white hairy bodies, and blue veins on their legs. Only two. And she passed me strange like a ghost. (*Thinking.*) I even went back to Roxbury. I got to stop that. Got to control my fears a little better than that. I get to seeing too much in dreams. So what difference does it make, Soledada, that you saw your aunt watching silently as those little dark boys put their hands up your dress? So you know who she is, what difference does it make now? And when I had my period that first time. And I was stuttering 'cause I thought I had done . . . (*thinks for a while*). So that's what it was about. Damn, they sure make it hard. They get you crazy real quick. Then they ask you to be a woman.

I see why he was taking dope. But I knew that anyway.

Just dreams though, can't be scared of dreams. (*Crawling back into bed.*) Too much life to be scared of.

If he comes home, I'll ask him who I am (*pause*). No, I won't.

[Darkness.]

Scene 24

Soledada and Celestina

[The house of Celestina. Celestina is dressed in a long black skirt and a very white silk blouse. Sole-dada is standing beside her as the scene opens. She seems genuinely confused as to what to do.]

SOLEDADA: I've seen you several times before on the street.

CELESTINA: I've seen you, too. You're very pretty.

SOLEDADA: Thank you, so are you.

CELESTINA: You have that nice look.

SOLEDADA: Oh?

CELESTINA: Why don't you sit down?

SOLEDADA: Celestina . . .

CELESTINA: Yes.

SOLEDADA: We're both black women, so we shouldn't be jealous of one another.

CELESTINA: Oh yeah.

SOLEDADA: I know that he cares for both of us although I . . . sometimes I think he prefers you.

CELESTINA: Listen, girl, let's get real for a minute. Black woman or no black woman, ain't no way in the world that you could dig me fucking your man.

SOLEDADA: I didn't say that I dug it. I accept it as a fact, though.

CELESTINA: All right. Now, about him preferring me to you, that's not real either. He's a man, men don't prefer, they just want. You know. They want it all—you, me, anybody else they see.

SOLEDADA: I suppose you're right.

CELESTINA: Damn right I'm right. I know all them jive-mother . . . (*stops herself*). Anyway, they all coming from the same place. Hey listen, I don't hardly want him.

SOLEDADA: We went away for a while, you know. I thought it would make him happier. Maybe loosen him up a little. It didn't.

CELESTINA: That's 'cause he's crazy. Didn't you know that? I mean, he's a pretty dude but he is crazy and he ain't about to change.

SOLEDADA: But he can be very gentle.

CELESTINA: Yeah, he can be gentle. I guess you still think it's possible to save somebody. Well, you can't.

SOLEDADA: You can't save anyone?

CELESTINA: You can't save a damn soul, no matter how bad you might want to.

SOLEDADA: Well, at least he's not strung out anymore.

CELESTINA: Yes, he does look better these days. He don't look so damn old.

SOLEDADA: I wonder what it is he wants. There must be something that would make him . . .

CELESTINA: You mean that would cool him out.

SOLEDADA: Yes.

CELESTINA: He wants to kill somebody.

SOLEDADA: (*choosing to ignore Celestina's last comment*) You're lucky, you know more about the streets than I do.

CELESTINA: Hell, ain't nothing lucky about that. I know too damn much. I wish I didn't know so much. They taught me too fast.

SOLEDADA: My parents tried to keep me from knowing.

CELESTINA: They did you a favor.

SOLEDADA: I don't know, I don't think so. Tell me, do you ever get scared?

CELESTINA: Scared, of what?

SOLEDADA: Of everything.

CELESTINA: No, ain't no sense being scared. (*She has her back turned when she says this. There is a pause and then she turns back to Soledada.*) That's not true. I stay scared. My nerves are always raggedy. That's why I drink. I don't want to think about nothing. (*Pause.*) He ain't in no trouble, is he?

SOLEDADA: Morose?

CELESTINA: Yeah. Ain't nobody looking for him?

SOLEDADA: Not that I know of. Why?

CELESTINA: I was just wondering.

SOLEDADA: Are you the one that scratches up his back so much? . . . You don't have to answer that.

CELESTINA: I don't know. I suppose I am. I get out there when I get into it. Why? Don't you cut him up? Listen, girl, don't worry. You the one he's going to be staying with.

[Celestina laughs and then Soledada joins her.]

[Darkness.]

Scene 25

[The stage light is neon blue. John Coltrane's "Meditation" is heard very low at first. The only stage prop necessary is a leather chair upon which El Cid is seated. The Chorus is shooting dice down-stage.]

EL CID: You're back.

MOROSE: Yes.

PEDRO: (*shooting*) Six.

EL CID: You lived well.

MOROSE: Very well.

EL CID: You sent one postcard from Holland and one from West Africa. You didn't even write anything on those.

MOROSE: No.

EL CID: There are a lot of women in the world, aren't there?

MOROSE: Yes, a lot.

EL CID: (*seeing he is getting no response*) You've had a chance to see how other people live. Have you learned anything?

MOROSE: Yes, people are asleep or hungry.

EL CID: Well, you saw that much anyway.

RAFAEL: Nine.

PEDRO: Shoot again.

EL CID: (*turning his back to Morose*) Did you see the Pyramids?

[142]

MOROSE: No, I saw who made the Pyramids.

EL CID: Oh, really.

PEDRO: Snake eyes.

RAFAEL: No, that's the Jew breathing at the door.

EL CID: Listen, I want you to get to know the business. I have a lot for you but I want you to earn it . . . as I did.

PEDRO: (*he hands Gongora the dice*) Here, old man, just throw them.

EL CID: If you think you want to be an architect I can arrange it so that . . .

MOROSE: (*calmly*) Turn around (*holding gun*).

EL CID: What! You're crazy. Put that away; you're not going to use that thing.

GONGORA: What did I shoot?

PEDRO: Six.

EL CID: Don't be stupid.

MOROSE: I am stupid.

[*The Chorus encircles El Cid.*]

EL CID: You're angry because of your mother. It wasn't my . . .

MOROSE: No, because of me.

EL CID: I can give you anything you want; anything.

MOROSE: No, you can't. Open your mouth.

EL CID: Morose!

[Morose sticks gun in his mouth and fires three times. Melibea runs on stage. The sound of Pedro's whip.]

MELIBEA: Uncle? You killed him.

PEDRO: No, I killed him. Shit, you act like I killed God or something.

RAFAEL: No, I killed him.

[They keep repeating this.]

MELIBEA: You can't, you can't get away. (*Suddenly realizing what she has said.*) I won't tell anyone.

MOROSE: Yes, you will (*in absolute calm*).

MELIBEA: No, I swear to God I won't say a word, just let me go.

PEDRO: She's sicker then he was. I should make her suck my dick. Come here, bitch.

MOROSE: No, go ahead, girl, you can do any damn thing you want to.

PEDRO: Are you crazy?

MOROSE: Go on.

[She runs offstage.]

[144]

PEDRO: Damn, at least let me whip her a little bit.

MOROSE: You sure dig that whip, don't you? Okay, people, you can go on.

GONGORA: What are you going to do?

MOROSE: It's already been done.

PEDRO: Yeah, well, I'm going to get the hell out of here. You got this.

GONGORA: One black body standing outside the world.

MOROSE: This is the way I walk, you see? Walk, move like this (*he fits word to act*). This is the way I breathe (*he takes deep breath*). Just like talking to God. The others don't understand just what I'm talking about. I like very much to walk, anywhere. Do you understand? Anywhere. It gives me the illusion that I'm free.

GONGORA: (*calling*) Morose! And first they will comprehend their sorrow, and then they will comprehend their rage. (*Center stage while Morose is in background.*) I would like . . . I would like to see the sunlight once more, just . . . (*screams*) give me some sunlight, give me some sun.

Please, God. Just once more. A blaze of color the way I dream it all over and over. Even if it's quickly, Lord. A knife blade of light. (*Ringing the gold bell which Morose gave him.*) A sky, no end to it, and if it burns me . . . all right then, I won't ask for more. But dammit, give me . . . give me . . . please give . . . Morose? (*He repeats over and over until he achieves ecstasy. The sound of John Coltrane's "Father, the Son and Holy Ghost" is heard, but dissolves into Thelonious Monk's*

"Misterioso." The stage is filled with total light.)

More, more light. Now more, more!

The Ascension

[Voice continuing until darkness and beyond it; Chorus exits as it entered.]

[Curtain.]